Who Was Who

Sex Changes

Edgar Cayce Legacy
Bible Playbook

Elyse Curtis, Ph. D.

Astral Projections
(A Division of Science of Light)

DEDICATION

To all those who seek this knowledge

Contents

Part III Sex Changes Through the Ages

Preface

Source of the Information
As the name implies, primary research source for *Sex Changes* from the *Who Was Who Edgar Cayce Legacy Bible Playbook*, is paralleled information from the Edgar Cayce files and the Bible drawing on the *Who Was Who: A Past Life Directory Based on the Edgar Cayce Discourses, Let There Be Light* and the individual *Who Was Who Bible Playbooks* in the series.

God's Book of Remembrances
In the Cayce discourses, source of the information, which was accessed and interpreted by the sleeping Edgar Cayce, was identified for two males (a fireman and an insurance agent) in the *Who Was Who* as the "Akashic records in God's book of remembrances" (3902-2), which is "the Book of Life:"

The Book of Life
The record that the individual entity itself writes upon the skein of time and space, through patience and is opened when self has attuned to the infinite, and may be read by those attuning to that consciousness. 2533-8

Biblically, the source of the information is identified as the same: "God's Book of Remembrances" (Mal. 3:16), "The Book of Life" (Rev. 20:12), record of the individual truthfully written in "the ark of his testament" in the temple of God in heaven (Rev. 11:19), which is opened when attuned to the spiritual level of consciousness.

Elyse Curtis, Ph.D.

Part I
The Body, Mind, Soul Trinity

►1◄
The Third Dimensional Body

In examining the physical gender, we begin with understanding that in this third dimension we are the trinity of body (the physical) mind (the mental), and soul (the spiritual). These three phases were explained to a male chiropractor:

> Do not confuse that which is of spirit, and soul, and that which is of physical-mental and that is of the material. Put proper evaluations upon all phases. 4083-1

Body, the material, is the earthly home of the soul: the individuality, the "I AM," the companion of spirit. Mind, the level where truth is faithfully recorded, is the builder: the maker.
Mind, Body, Soul
Mind is represented in the Godhead as the Christ, the Son, the Way. The Father is represented in the earth as the body. The soul is all of those attributes that manifest in the body. 4083-1

Biblically, this is expressed by the Christ, the Son as: "I am the way, the truth, and the life: no man comes to the Father, but by me." (John 14: 6) and "I and *my* Father are one" (John 10:30).

1

Soul First

As we would give, an entity body-mind was first a soul before it entered into material consciousness. 4083-1

►2 ◄
The Spiritual Body

Before the soul entered into material consciousness, "the spirit of God (Elohiym: Gods), moved upon the face of the water" (Gen. 1:2) and brought forth "the true light, which lights *every man* that comes into the world." (John 1:9)

Gods of the Universe

Confirmation of the plurality and identity of God (Elohiym: Gods), the Creator, is addressed in the Cayce Discourses and the Bible:

Forget not that it has been said correctly that the Creator, the Gods and the God of the Universe, speak to man through this individual self. 3744-5

Biblically, Daniel (called Belteshazzar) was said to have the "spirit of the holy gods" (Dan.4:8, 18).

The answer to what is meant by the Gods of the Universe: "that force referred to as the gods, rulers of the elements," was clarified for a female listed as a secretary in the *Who Was Who* as:

fire, earth, air, water. These are the NATURAL elements in the physical plane, and as the forces of these have the influence as the SPIRIT of the air. ...The SPIRIT of each! 288-27

Spirit

A glimpse of these early beginnings as Spirit is in the *Who Was Who* entries for those whose first appearance as Spirit is listed:

Spirit - Among those chosen as messengers to all the realm in the beginning, when the Sons of God came together for appearance of man in earth plane. (0137)

Spirit - Among the first who came to view earth's sphere before the planet was habitable to human life. Passed on to other spheres about earth. (0228)

Spirit - When earth forces were called into existence. Present when the Sons of God came together for advent of man. (0234)

Spirit - Among the first who came into material activity, into consciousness, into awareness of the relationships of physical man to the Creative Forces. (0257)

Spirit/Sound

Mmuum [sound] - Spirit entity able to be in or out of body before habitation of perfect physical form. (0436)

The final creation in Genesis (1:26-27): man made in the image of God (Elohiym: Gods), the invisible God (Col. 1:15), was the spiritual body: the soul.

►3◄
Soul: The Image of God

"God *is* not a man...neither the son of man" (Num. 23:19) "God is spirit" (John 4:24)

The soul, the companion of spirit, as the biblical image, not the body, was clarified for a male listed as a retired professor in the *Who Was Who*:

For as each soul not the body but the soul is the image of the Maker. 2246-1

The image of God, the spiritual body, contained the total positive/negative, male/female forces: the twin soul that would be separated later:

"So God created man in his own image, in the image of God created he him; male and female created he them." (Gen. 1:26-27)

Twin Souls

An instance of twin souls appear in the *Who Was Who* as "A Voice" when the Father gave the first indwelling of man, before the male/female separation:

Voice Over Many Waters [0288 & 0294] as one in mind, soul, spirit, body

Thought Projection

In another instance before the male/female separation, a male pianist in the *Who Was Who* first appeared as a **"Thought projection"** that contained both sexes in one body and sought to be both, but was not very successful at either. (5056)

Separation of the forces as genders would take place after *formation* of the physical body by the Lord God, the Maker, who is identified to a male student in the *Who Was Who* as One Source:

►4◄
The Master Soul: The Lord God

"The Lord thy God is ONE" [Deut. 6:4, Mk.12:29] and all power, all force emanates from that One Source. 391-4

The Lord God who appeared in Gen. 2:1-4 on the seventh day while God (Elohiym: Gods) rested, was biblically identified as: the "I AM THAT I AM" (Exo. 3:14), the Master Soul, the Christ soul (John 8:58), the first begotten Son of God, "the image of the invisible God, the firstborn of every creature" (Col. 1:15), the Word that was with God and was God, in whom was life that was the light of man (John 1:1-4).

This great I AM THAT I AM as the individual I AM was affirmed to a female:

That I AM then within self, responding to the **I AM THAT I AM**, [Exo. 3:14] is indeed the psychic or soul or of the soul self. 1376-1

This oneness as the source was reiterated to another female listed as a former concert singer in the *Who Was Who*:

For all souls were created in the one…ALL souls are from one. 1770-2

The Physical Body
"And the LORD God had not caused it to rain upon the earth, and there was not a man to till the ground. But there went up a *mist* from the earth, and watered the whole face of the ground." (Gen. 2:5-6)

The Breath of Life
"And the LORD God formed man of the *dust* of the ground, and breathed into his nostrils the *breath of life*; and man became a living soul." (Gen. 2:7)

Elements of Body and Soul
The physical body was formed from the elements of "earth," the dust of the ground: *adamah*: "redness" from *adam*: "to show blood," and "water," the mist, while the soul, which contained the total force, entered with the element "air," the breath of life.

The element "water" on which spirit moves, was the vehicle for the five-point projection, the streams of spiritual consciousness of the five divisions of the race that represented the five senses.

"And a river went out of Eden to water the garden; and from thence it was parted, and became into four heads." (Gen. 2:10)

►5◄
The Five-point Projection

When the earth brought forth the seed in her season, and man came in the earth plane as the lord of that in that sphere, man appeared in five places then at once – the five senses, the five reasons, the five spheres, the five developments, the five nations. 5748-1

Adamic Man
Adam...appeared as five in one. 364-11

It was only after the river parted into the four heads and went out of Eden to water the garden and the Lord God formed the animals, so that *the man* would not be alone, that the name Adam appeared (Gen. 2:19).

As these took form, by the gratifying of their own desire for that as builded or added to the material conditions, they became hardened or set much in the form of the existent human body of the day, with that of color as partook of its surroundings much in the manner as the chameleon in the present. 364-3

Race, Sense and Gender
The five nations, the five divisions of the race developed physically according to their environments. The colors into which they evolved were incidental, as they were "all of one, or one race, or no races" as explained to a 23 year-old male in the *Who Was Who*.

Each sense being vital to the One body in the material plane was explained by Paul in his letters (Rom. 12. 4-5, 1 Cor. 6.15, 12.12, 18-27, and Eph. 5.30). Rather, it was the attributes of the senses that the five divisions represented by which they should be identified.

►6◄
Separation of the Genders

Separation of the forces, the male/female polarities, the genders, the twin souls, into two separate physical bodies (Gen. 2:21-25) after naming of the animals (identifying the emotions), came because of mental/emotional desire for companionship, followed by desire to procreate physically.

Adam, as given first discerned that from himself, not of the beasts about him, could be drawn WAS drawn that which made for the propagation OF beings IN the flesh that made for that companionship as seen by creation in the material worlds about same. 364-5

Journey of the Sexes
The five Adams, progenitors of the five divisions of the human race, began as both forces in one body that later separated leading to "the fall," "the curse," which pre-shadowed physical "death:" the point at which the return of the soul, the individuality as separate personalities in other bodies was set into motion as explained to a female listed as a stenographer in the *Who Was Who:*

Individuality
The Lord thy God is one [Deut. 6:4, Mk. 12:29]. The self as an individual entity, body, mind and soul is one. The soul is a child of God, or a thought, a corpuscle in the heart of God. 3376-2

Will

Yet the entity, thine own soul, has been given a will to use the attributes of soul, mind and body to thine own purposes. Thus as the individual entity applies self in relationship to those facts, the entity shows itself to be a true child or a wayward child, or a rebellious child, of the Creative Force or God. 3376-2

Individuality/Personality

Individuality, the soul identity that is eternal, is layered by the personality of each separate appearance, whatever gender force it incarnates as. This is explained in the lesson on Destiny in the Search for God[5] series to the original Study Group (Norfolk #1) whose members appear in the *Who Was Who*: and the *Search for God Bible Playbook* series:

That force, that power, which manifests itself in separating or as separate forces and influences in the earth, continue to enter; and then change; continuing to pour in and out. 262-88

Clarification of that statement requested by the study group explained it further:

Just as has been explained in how spirit sought projecting; chose to enter that as had been the creation of the Father as manifestations, that still is as manifestations; and thus enters, leaves, enters, leaves, or **incarnates** through the lessons gained in each experience. 262-99

Biblically, this pouring in and out is noted in Micah's messianic prophecy of the coming Ruler out of Bethlehem "whose goings forth have been from of old, from everlasting." (Mic. 5.2)

Part II
Sex Change Incarnations

►7◄
The Process
That there is a structure to the "goings forth" mentioned by
the prophet Micah was alluded to for a female seamstress in
the *Who Was Who*:

We Do Not Enter By Chance
For the entity comes, not by chance, but purposefully, that
there might be the more perfect preparation for the soul to
be as that for which the Lord, the Maker of the heavens
and the earth intended and prepares a way for same. -
4055-2

Individual souls can manifest as either gender in various
lives changing from one life to the other according to the
development needed.

Purpose of the incarnation given to a female in the *Who
Was Who* that had been a male in Rome during the Greek
Classical period, was: "The meeting of self to blot out
resentments." 2872-3

Because the soul is eternal and continually meets self,
entering to deal with past actions is an opportunity. This
was affirmed to a female in the *Who Was Who* that had
been a male during the Exodus:

Do analyze self and the ideas and ideals of self. Know
that the entrance into a material manifestation is not
merely to gratify self nor to be more highly spoken of

than your neighbor, or to gratify appetites, but rather it is the opportunity for the individual entity to manifest the source of life or God. And they who fail, do so to their own undoing. 3285-2

That we do not enter by chance was also explained to a female in the *Who Was Who* that had been a male in Greece when Xenophon was leader in the eastern land:

For, it is not by chance that an entity enters at some particular period or experience, but that it may be fulfilled in that promise, He hath not willed that any soul should perish, but hath with each temptation prepared a way [2 Pet. 3:9], a manner. 2331-1

The way prepared as explained to a female sales personnel manager in the *Who Was Who* appears to be on-going and automatic depending on the actions as described in Ecclesiastes where we are compared to trees:

As The Tree Falls, So Does It Lie
Because one passes on, the activity does not cease. "As the tree falls, so does it lie" [Eccl. 11:3], saith the Maker and Giver of life. So does the light, so does the nature of an individual. For the beginnings in the next experiences are ever tempered by how sincere the purpose was of the entity in the experience before. 5260-1

The imagery of the tree was also used to explain this to the Search for God Study Group

For each experience in the earth is as a schooling, is as an experience for the soul. For how gave He? He is the vine and ye are the branches, [John 15:1-2] or He IS the source and ye are the trees. 262-99

As the tree falls so does it lie [Eccl. 11:3]. THERE it

begins when it has assimilated, when it has applied in SPIRITUAL reaction that it has gained. 262-99

►8◄
The Individual Records

Where her past-life information came from was also given to the female sales personnel manager in the *Who Was Who*:

The Skein of Time and Space
In giving the interpretations of the records, these are taken from those impressions which are made upon the skein of time and space by the physical and mental activities of this entity. 5260-1

Why Certain Records Were Chosen
That only those lives relevant to development of the individual soul were chosen from their records was explained to two females in the *Who Was Who*.

One had been male during the Crusades:

While not all may be given, these are chosen that indicate how and why such influences are a part of the latent and manifested urges in the present.

For, each entity is today what it is because of what it was yesterday, and because of what it did about the creative influence in relationships to the ideals chosen or set. 2572-1

One had been male during the time of Zenophon in Greece:

In giving the interpretations of the records as we find them here, these are chosen from same with the desire that this be a helpful experience for the entity in determining that purpose for which the entity entered this experience in the present sojourn; and thus fulfill that as may make for a growth in the soul urge. 2331-1

Why Sex Change

Answer to the question of why a female in the *Who Was Who* had been a female wild animal trainer among the barbarians, the "wild" people, in the Arabian incarnation during the Ra-Ta period in Egypt, was because of an incarnation prior to that in Egypt:

That incarnation had been an opportunity, which occurred from *desire* brought over from the previous incarnation in Egypt. At that time, when the Nile emptied into the Atlantic, before the mountains rose in the south, she organized families for common interest and protection against the beasts. Next time she chose to tame the wild beasts.

Why Some Change and Others Don't

A male in the *Who Was Who* from Pensacola, Florida, who had been male in all of his incarnations and asked why some and not others changed sex, was given basically the same answer: *spiritual desire*. The answer also shed some light on gender in-between during the planetary sojourns:

That is from the SPIRITUAL desire. Now - DESIRE may be given in a varied form or manner, and in some conditions appear only as wish, or as an expression of a SENSING from within. In this there is seen as to HOW that the desire of an individual would BRING them in under the environ of male or female, while one may appear in the earth as male or female as a regular or at intervals, according to the DEVELOPMENT. In the same SPHERE - that is, in other planets there may be an entirely different sex, BY the desire or that builded, see? 311-3

Can One Gender Really Understand The Other?
Answer to this question was given to a female in the *Who Was Who* that had incarnated continually as a female: in the Ra-Ta period in Egypt, the Early Christian Era, in Palestine, with first settlers in Early America, and in 1894:

> For here again we find an entity every whit woman, not having changed its sex in its experiences in the earth. No wonder the entity doesn't understand men, nor men understand the entity. They cannot think in the same channel, not having experienced that which is the prompting urge from a first cause and a twig or a rib out of the first cause, for these are rarely considered in their correct relationships as man to woman. 3379-2

►9◄
Curious Entries

Among the sex change incarnations in the *Who Was Who* in the historic eras, some stand out because of the impact the sex change had in future lives, or the special information or circumstances included. Some are even startling to the one conveying the information from the records.

Three from the *Who Was Who* that stand out in that category because of special information imparted before the incarnations were given are one for a male supervisor, one for a female insurance agent, and one for a social worker:

One in Twenty-Three Men
One of the most curious entries in the sex change category was for a male supervisor born in Philadelphia, Pennsylvania, 06/23/1913 that was prefaced with: "This is funny, there are only twenty-three other people born on June 23, 1913 in the U.S.A. **that are men.**" 5725-1

"In giving the interpretations of the records of the entity here, as we find, it is rather a problem with the entity in choosing activity, owing to urges because of the **tendency of feminine activity in the entity's characteristics**." 5725-1

▶ Now He Fears Both Sexes
Male to Female to Twice to Male

After life as a musician in ancient Egypt, he was next a female in France during the Crusades:

Juean Horellett [Female] - Engaged to Crusader, ignorant of marital relationships and duties feared matrimony, grew to hate opposite sex, fears not removed until older, fear of both men and women became part of consciousness - 5725-1 M 30 -2

The next incarnation was as a female in Early America before returning as a male in 1913.

What Records!
The combination of lives viewed in the records for a female insurance agent born in Iatt, Grant Parish, Louisiana, 03/01/1897 invoked a startling response when being given:

Yes, we have the entity here and those records and what records! As has been and is the experience of the entity in the present consciousness in the earth's plane, these produce in the present very exceptional characteristics. 3481-2

She had been a female close to the young king in Egypt during the Ra-Ta period and a companion of a priest, versed in laws, in the Holy Land when they were going into captivity, and was next a male in early America during period of the French "lost cause," settling in portions of

Alabama, Mississippi and Louisiana before the one in 1897:

Elisha Eli [Male] Among French returning to France, remained, became business man, gained materially by bringing others under influence, created mental problem that must be met by finding ideal: - 3481-2 F 47-3

Her exceptional characteristics were not easily interpreted by her acquaintances, but those who knew her best loved her idiosyncrasies gained from past experiences, one of which was unique:

►**Now She Can Keep a Secret from Her Husband**
Female to Female to Male to Female

A most capable entity and that which may be said of the entity in the present sex may be said of few women: she can keep a secret even from her own husband, as she did to her undoing.

We would, then, rather give the entity the ideal manner in which the abilities may be applied, and thus the entity must choose for itself. 3481-2

►**Bible Playbook◄**

The Lord, Thy God, Is One
In the application, then, first know what ye believe, spiritually, and who is the author of thy ideal. Remember there are not authors, it is not plural. For the Lord, thy God, is one [Deut. 6:4, Mk. 12:29]. Don't forget it! He's not multiple; there are helpers, yes, but each individual soul is meant to help. 3481-2

Know In Whom Ye Believe

Know, then, in whom ye believe and in what ye believe [2Tim.1:12], spiritually; then know what is thy idea and also thy ideal mentally. For mind is the builder. For it partakes both of materiality and eternity and spirituality.

These know, for these are true. The results in thy experience materially should be, will be when ye are assured, pleasing first in the sight of God and harmonious in thine own experience.3481-2

Choose Thou - The Law of the Lord Is Perfect

As indicated, we have shown thee a more excellent way, choose thou! [Jos. 24:15] For the law of the Lord is perfect [Psa. 19:7] and is not altered by man's wishes. The law of the Lord keepeth one in the right way [1 Cor. 12:31] when man makes his will one with the Father. 3481-2

►10◄
Proof?

Three entries in the sex-change category in the *Who Was Who* contained information on where to find records of those particular lives.

An unusual bit of information concerning the name change was given to a female that could be researched to confirm the sex-changed life:

Later the entity's name was changed to George Maurier, and there may be found among the old records of that New Amsterdam or the Philadelphia land the older records of how the joinings of those people of the simple faith, of the simpler things in the material, influenced the greater number during that sojourn. 0764-1

►Name Is In Puritan Records
Female Three times to Male to Female

A female Christian of French ancestry born in New Orleans, Louisiana, 04/09/1895, who had been an Atlantean female in Egypt during the Ra-Ta period, a Grecian female in Persia during the Uhjltd period and a female associated with those in household of Herod, who became a friend of Pilate's wife and Holy Women when The Master walked in the earth, was a male in early Philadelphia and New York when there were changes in New Amsterdam:

George Maurier (nee Jean Du Maurierten) [Male] Mutineer with expedition, sought to destroy things that brought burdens to others, fell in love, joined those of the simple faith 0764-1 F 33-4

In the present from that sojourn there is the love of the eastern land; and the ways that pertain to mystery stories, to the activities of individuals, become as a portion of the entity's activity in the present. 0764-1

►Bible Playbook◄

Seek the LORD While He May Be Found
Seek the Lord while He may be found! [Isa. 55:6] Make thy paths straight! 0764-1

Proclaim the Acceptable Year of the LORD
Turn ye while ye may, for the acceptable year of the Lord is at hand! [Isa. 61:2] And to the entity these words RING as something that takes hold upon the inner self. 0764-1

Answer to her question whether she should continue helping in the spiritual lives of others, was:

The Pearl of Great Price

As indicated, as ye give out what has been the motivating influence in thine own experience, ye may make in the experience of others that which will make each soul find the pearl of great price [Mat. 13:45-46]. 0764-1

The other entry was given concerning where the records could be found concerning activities during the period of the witch hunts:

> And there may be found, in that particular influence and surrounding, a record of those activities there. 0892-1

►Records of Activities are in Salem
Female Three Times (?) to Male to Female

A female physician born in Simsbury, Connecticut, 09/27/1882, whose occupations in previous incarnations as a Ruler in Atlantis, town clerk in Persia during the Uhjltd period, physician, barber, clerk, and footman in Rome during the Early Christian era all suggested that she had been male, was definitely identified as male in the one in Salem: Providence Town, Massachusetts when they were experiencing outer-influence in material expressions

> **Abanethey [Male]** Minister, questioned about own household, then called into question many of own household, later attempted to correct what had been set in motion, overridden by those in authority, suffered physically. 0892-1 F 52-4

In the present from that experience, such influences - such experiences that have had to deal with individuals, whether in vision, in spirit, in dream, in metaphysical, in the esoteric and esoteric influences - become questionings first, of studying when apparent, of making for a portion or partial application when found to be of those natures that answer to that something builded innately within the self from that sojourn. 0892-1

Abilities/Advice
As to the abilities of the entity in the present, and that to which it may attain, and how:

First in self find what are the promptings for thy activities, in relationships to thy fellow man. Know thy ideal; not of mental or material import but of the spiritual. For MIND is the builder, the Spirit is the motivative force and is the turning of self to the things of the spirit; then may the promptings make for that in the experience in whatever direction the activities may be taken, to be of a CONSTRUCTIVE nature in the experience of the entity. And only these bring peace, harmony, joy of life, of service, of activity. 0892-1

The third entry also concerned the Salem Witch Hunt period and concerned what might be considered an historic landmark:

►A Commemorative Slab - Salem
...there may be found as yet the monuments or the little slab in the outer portion of Salem, in what is called Massachusetts, of Allen, the minister to this church. 509-1

Female Twice to Male to Female
Twice to Male to Female

A female born in Santa Rosa or Petaluma, California, 09/24/1868, who had been a female in pre-historic America, which influenced much of history, and in Ancient Egypt during the Ra-Ta period, was a Grecian male in Persia and female again in Palestine as sister of the Virgin Mary, in Rome during the Early Christian era sacrificed at

age 16, and again as a male in Salem before the female one
in 1868:

Allen **[Male]** Minister, persecuted, banished for
attempting to clarify conditions of those who had visions
(there may be found as yet the monuments or the little
slab in the outer portion of Salem, in what is called
Massachusetts, of Allen, the minister to this church.) -
0509-1 F 65-6

Advice on her abilities in the present and how to attain was:

◄Bible Playbook►

Press on to the Mark of the Higher Calling
As to how, using that thou hast in hand day by day **press
on to the mark of the higher calling** [Phil. 3:1] as thou
hast seen in Him, and in the souls of those that guarded
Him even when He was tempted in the earth. 509-1

The Body Is the Temple of the Living God
So may the life in the present experience bring to those
whom the entity, whom the soul may contact, the
knowledge that God is in His holy temple within the body
of each and every being, and we may worship there in spirit
and in truth; that the body indeed may be the temple of the
living God, [1 Cor. 6:19] that He may indeed walk among
men, that He may indeed talk face to face with His
brethren, even as He did as He walked in Galilee. So may
the life, so may the experience of life; for Life itself is of
God, of mercy, of hope, of patience, of truth, of light itself.
Even as the soul has manifested in and among its fellow
man, may it bring step by step that understanding that He
IS. Let Him have HIS way with thee. 509-1

Answer to the request for a detailed explanation on just
how she could be of greater service to mankind in the rest

of her life was:

In **doing that the heart and the hands find to do**. [Eccl. 9:10] 509-1

Be Not Weary In Well-Doing

Be not weary in well-doing; [Gal. 6:9, 2Thes. 3:13] for, as has been given, that thou hast accomplished has been accepted in His sight. Then, grow not weary. Keep the mind and the heart busy in making known the love of the Christ child in the hearts, in the souls of those that are seeking so much. As the soul of this entity has found, there is in the present the greater seeking for the knowledge that is so simple that in its simplicity man, in his self-righteousness, stumbles over day by day that which if taken and nourished in his heart and soul would bring that peace and harmony and glory that makes known the love of the Christ child in the hearts of men. So, in doing this, in being led by Him day by day, may the greater glory and peace and harmony and understanding come to this soul in this experience. 509-1

►11◄
Patterns

Another entry in which the person's sex change life placed her in England during a time of change was part of her soul pattern that would continue in her life time:

As indicated, in periods when changes were being wrought, the entity has entered the earth even as a pattern. Changes are due to be wrought in the earth through the period of the entity's sojourn. 3648-1

►A Continuing Pattern of Earth Changes
Female to Female to Male to Female Twice

A female born in Philadelphia, Pennsylvania, 05/14/1916, who had been females in the Ra-Ta period in Egypt and the Uhjltd period in Persia, was next a male in England when the common people rebelled against the Church:

> **Lord Chesterberg [male]** - Among those following the one (Cromwell [2903]), who rebelled against the king, brought better interpretations of purpose - 3648-1 F 27 - 3

The Pattern
Then, seek the associations and the companionships through which ye may contribute to these changes that may have as great effect upon the future as ye have had through the other periods of activity; and ye will be creating for thine own individuality, for thine own entity's influence, that which will be a continued growth. 3648-1

Following the incarnation in England, he was a female during the American Civil War, a period of change in the United States, and again in the one in Philadelphia in 1916 following WWI where she also experienced the changes in the 1920's, the Great depression, and WWII.

In response to her query in 1944 of how to know individuals with whom she should be associated, she was given an answer from Paul's letter to the Romans that is applicable to all, plus a personal clue:

▶ Bible Playbook ◀

My Spirit Bears Witness with Your Spirit
For there is the answer, "My spirit beareth witness with thy spirit" [Rom. 8:16]. And his birthday will be the fourteenth of October. 3648-1

▶ Delayed Pattern and Soul Growth
Female Three Times to Male to Female

One of the females in the sex change category in the *Who Was Who* had been one of the wives left behind during the Crusades, which is an indication that she had been made to wear a chastity belt. Although her sex change was her next life as a male in Early America, the impact of that experience during the Crusades was a pattern that was to be met in her present life:

The entity was among the wives who were left, and were mistrusted as to their relationships with others. These experiences brought for the entity a great deal of condemnation, upon others as well as upon self; and yet in the latter portion of that sojourn the entity GAINED, - for it trusted not in self nor in others but rather in Him who is able to keep those forces, those activities, in that way - in the relationships with others - as to bring harmony, peace and understanding. 2116-2

In the experience the entity gained. In the present we find relationships both material and filial, in which questions as to those things that were pronouncements through that sojourn are being met within the present. 2116-2

The information that she was given was not chosen by random, but for soul growth:

In giving the interpretations of the records as we find them here, these are chosen from same with the desire that this be a helpful experience for the entity in determining that purpose for which the entity entered this experience in the present sojourn; and thus fulfill that as may make for a growth in the soul urge. 2116-2

For, each soul manifests that it may become a channel through which there may be expressed the ideal which is set in creative energies and forces as manifested in the man Jesus. So may each soul grow in grace, in knowledge, in understanding. For, His promises are sure; to those who walk in that way in which the life, the manifestations in relationships to others, bring hope and creative forces of a spiritual import in the experience of self and others. 2116-2

◄Bible Playbook►

Take My Yoke and Learn of Me
Such may at times require sacrifices upon the part of self, yet KNOWING WHY, and the purpose for such, these should become not as burdens, but as He gave, "Take my yoke upon you and learn of me, for my burden is light"{Mat. 11:29-30] and easy to those who seek to know His way. 2116-2

Answer to the query about her abilities in the present, that to which it may attain and how was:

He That Would Be The Greatest...
Remember, "He that would be the greatest among you will be the servant of all" [Mat. 20:27, Mat. 23:11, Mk. 10:44]. 2116-2

In Patience Ye Possess Your Soul
Be patient, for in patience ye possess your soul. [Luke 21:19] 2116-2

Answer to her query of what is behind her feeling of depression and discouragement was not to condemn self or others followed by quotes from James and Acts:

Giver of All Good and Perfect Gifts
In Him Ye Live and Move
As indicated, these feelings arise from the self-effacement that is self-condemnation. Condemn not others, and not thyself. Leave that thou canst not do nor understand to

HIM, who is the Giver of all good and perfect gifts [Jas. 1:17]. For in Him ye live and move and have thy being [Acts 17:28]. Do not engage, in mind or body, in that which brings condemnation to self. 2116-2

►12◄
Chose to Enter Purposely

In the sex-change category in the *Who Was Who*, two females: a linotype operator and a lecturer and author, who had made it to Arcturus, which is "the way, the door out of this system" chose purposely to return.   The lecturer also purposely determined to change gender and did:

►Determined To Be Male Next Time and Was
Female Five Times to Male to Female Three Times

A female author/lecturer born in Dayton, Washington, 05/15/1899, who had been a female in Atlantis, in Egypt during the Ra-Ta period, in Peru, in Damacus during the captivity, and in Persia when Babylon was being founded by Semiramis:

But from this experience there came the determinations of the entity to appear next in the opposite sex, because of the relationships brought by the activities of Semiramis in the Persian activities. 2454-3

In the next experience, her desire was manifested; she was a male in Rome when there were changes and attempts to sail to other lands

Romolonoun [Male] Sailor in charge of fleet to Ireland and England, gained, through its journeys in the earth; though he had disturbances in overcoming the tendencies that are often accredited to those of its own present sex. - 2454-3 F 43 – 6

Following that experience as a male, he changed sex and appeared as female four more times: in Palestine when The Master walked in the earth, Early America, when settlers came from Ireland, time of the Gold Rush, and in 1899.

► Bible Playbook ◄

You Shall Give Account of Every Word Spoken
As indicated, the material appearances have been quite varied; yet very sincere, very stern in most of the activities in the earth. Thus, in its relationships with others in the present, the entity is one qualified to interpret most any phase of an individual experience. Thus others will listen. 2454-3

Hence the entity should be guarded, not as to what it would say or as to whether it would say, but as to what and how and when it says. Not that the entity speaks too often, but just remember that others listen and recall "Ye shall give an account of every word that is spoken" [Rom. 14:12]. For in the speaking, thy words are given power. 2454-3

The other female, who entered purposely was said to have unusual abilities:

In giving the interpretations of the records, these we choose from same with the desire that this may prove a helpful experience for the entity. For, we have unusual abilities in this entity, dependent upon how the entity may use same as to whether these become hindrances in the material and mental life, or whether they grow to be useful for enlightening and helpful experiences for others. 5259-1

►Now She Can See Through Men
Female to Female Twice to Male to Female

The entity was among that group, and thus a man, or in the opposite sex. Thus in the present, the peculiar feeling toward sex and men, and as to how the entity can see through them and what they are thinking almost. It's because you were one, not because you're so wise. These are the urges. 5259-1

A female linotype operator born on a farm near Henry, South Dakota, 10/18/1897, was a Princess, an interpreter of activities to be sent to other lands from the Golden Land [Gobi] in Egypt during the Ra-Ta period, a female sand reader, soothsayer in Persia during the Uhjltd period, and a female who enlarged upon activities using the holy of holies, ephod, and Urim and Thummim in England during the activities of daughter of King Hezekiah from Holy Land, was a male in Pre-Columbian America when early groups were traveling from east toward the area that became South Dakota with Eric the Red (982 A.D.)

Esten Esten [Male] - With group that settled in Area that became Wisconsin for a time, studied with indigenous medicine men - 5259-1 F 46- 4

Bible Playbook- Advice/Warnings

First, find self in those directions taken and given in Exodus19:5; Deuteronomy 30; St. John 14 and 15 particularly. And then use as the model, as the symbol, the lines of the hand, to interpret for individuals their idiosyncrasies, their shortcomings, their abilities and such, but do NOT prognosticate. 5259-1

As indicated, do not listen to voices, or rappings outside of self; do NOT use incense or music or automatic writing, for too many may desire to use this entity. 5259-1

Do interpret from that which may be gained from these: [Exo. 19:5; Deut. 30; St. John 14, 15]. These interpret within self; apply them in self. 5259-1

►13◄
Unusual Sex Change Entries

The variation of sex in different incarnations, which resulted in the individual having the ability to love, but not inclined to be affectionate, made for an unusual record:

> What an unusual record, the entity having been a man more than once! thus an individual entity who is in its characteristics and mental processes quite efficient and at times quite sufficient unto itself. 4067-1

►Repulsed by and Attracted to Opposite Sex
Female to Male to Female to Male to Female

> The entity finds self with the ability to love, yes but rather not inclined to be affectionate in any way. These are tendencies or characteristics that are a part of the entity's experience because of the variation of the sex. We find that these contribute in many ways to the abilities of the entity yet in many of the emotions, as has been the experience of the entity, have been at times quite confusing; as the entity's emotion towards its own sex under certain conditions, as well as the repulsion and attraction to the opposite sex. 4067-1

A female social worker born in Sullivan, Illinois 10/30/1901 had seesawed from male to female sex changes in incarnations: from female in Egypt during the Ra-Ta period to male in the Holy Land during the return from captivity to female in the Holy Land during the period of the Judges to male in France during the time of preparation for the Crusades to another life as a male in Early America during the revolutionary period followed by the female one in Illinois - 4067-1 F 42

Ability
The social life, the social experiences of individuals and groups as related to their relationships to others of the entity's own sex or the opposite sex are of the universal nature. These at times, bring wonderments and confusions to the entity. 4067-1

...For the complexity of the individual attaining to that consciousness from which either of the sexes may be judged, brings rather an impelling or compelling influence in the experience of the entity in the present. 4067-1

Attributes Acquired
In addition to the ones that stood out because the records were startling to the one conveying the information, other entries in the *Who Was Who* stood out because of the abilities, attributes or innate urges acquired from changing gender.

►Now She Knows What Men Think
Female to Female to Male to Female

Hence the unusual circumstance oft in the present concerning its activities and associations with those of the opposite sex. Yet the entity UNDERSTANDS, knows almost more what men think than men do themselves, in company or companionship with the entity! 2610-1

A female nurse born in Ogdensburg, New York, 08/26/1898, whose first soul activity in earth had been as a female in Egypt during the Ra-Ta period, returned as a female again in Palestine when The Master walked in the earth, then as a male Crusader in France before returning as a female:

Pierre LaVeptee [Male] Crusader - With return from the false hopes aroused by others, determined to leave, exterminate, or to hold no feelings regarding same [the experience of being in opposite sex], gained the hard way - 2610-1 F 43-3

◄**Bible Playbook**►

He That Would Be the Greatest...
First, analyze thyself, thy purpose in the earth. Know this is not by chance, but for definite activities, definite opportunities for service. And he that would be the greatest among thy brethren will be the servant of all [Mat. 20:27, 23:11, Mk. 10:44]. 2610-1

►**Masculine Thought Will Be Manifested**
Female Three Times to Male to Female Twice

And in the present those experiences and expressions will be seen as a part of the entity's development, in that its masculine thought will be a manifestation in the early portion of its experiences, the desire to know the whys of life. 1566-3

A two-year-old female born in Norfolk, Virginia, 03/02/1938, who had been females in Egypt during the Ra-Ta period, in Persia during the Uhjltd period, in Palestine from the expectancy to the early Christian era, and in Greece when first male and beginning of females were being used in song, dance and calisthenics was next a male in France during the early period of the Louis' when there were the greater entertainments:

Cheveaux [Male] Entertainer to king as the "upper secretary" in counsel - 1566-3 F 2-5

Following that incarnation, he re-entered as females in Early Tidewater and in the one in 1938.

▶ **Acquired Reasoning from Male Incarnation**
Female to Female to Male to Female Twice

From the application of the entity as the man during that sojourn, we find in the present experience the abilities to sway others not only by its reasoning, not only by its abilities to make practical applications of mental and spiritual laws but to make them practical in the everyday life. 1554-2

A female translator born in Guvisy, France, 01/24/1891, who had been a female in Egypt during the Ra-Ta period and a princess/teacher during the period of Saneid in India whose basis of teaching was the Golden Rule [Mat. 7:12] was next a male in Greece following schools of thought of Plato and Socrates, and changing to teachings of Cistus:

Grecian [Male] - Leader in school of thought pertaining to closer relationship between material gains and bodily benefits, supplied materials for artists and sculptors - 1554-2 F 74 -3

Following that incarnation he changed sex and was female in France during gathering for The Crusades and in the one in 1891.

▶ **Now She Has Feminine and Masculine Traits**
Male to Female Three Times

Here again we find that the entity has changed back and forth in its sex, and - while very feminine - the entity would appear in many respects very masculine. 3345-1

A female High School Teacher born in Staffordshire, England, 02/08/1896, who had been the biblical character *Canaan [Male] - Son of Ham, next appeared as a female in the Incal Land when the Atlanteans journeyed to set up what later became known as Incal activities:

Esema [Female] Companion of leader who set custom and rituals following destruction of Atlantis - 3345-1 F 47-2
Innate Urge
To know those things that are to many classed as unknowable, to do those odd or unusual things that few others of the entity's sex have been able to do, becomes an innate urge and is the field of activity for the entity. 3345-1

Following that incarnation she was female during the Exodus when the Midianites were being destroyed by Eleazar, in Rome during the persecutions of the church, and in the one in 1896.

▶ Has Doubts Because of Experience
Female to Male to Female Three Times

Thus the innate longing in the present activities of the entity for new scenes, new fields, new endeavors, new thrills, new activities; and still that which makes for sociability with the opposite sex, and yet doubting most of them from its own experience. 2011-1

A female bank clerk born in Pittsburgh, Pennsylvania, 07/31/1902, who had been a female adept in archeology, astrology, geometry, and activities for emissaries during the Ra-Ta period in Egypt, was next a male in Norway during the period of the Norse voyages:

Zebun [Male] Shipbuilder, seaman, explorer searching for new lands and strange sights - 2011-1 (3) F 37 - 2

Following that experience he was female in Rome when faiths were being tested, in America during the Revolution and in the one in 1902.

►Gained Ability to Be Hale Fellow Well Met
Female to Female to Male to Female Twice

In the experience, the entity gained and lost, and yet the activities which make for the ability to be for the hale soul, or hale fellow well met in those activities, arise from those experiences. 5260-1

A female sales personnel mgr, born in Ashley, North Dakota, 07/01/1893, who had been females in Atlantis when there was breaking up of the land, and in Persia during the Uhjltd period where she gained as head instructor of school, was next a male in France during period when there was the gathering for crusades:

Aaron Ludwig [Male] - Crusader active in the ideals of those who offered themselves for helpful influences to a cause and purpose, did not apply same application to the associations or companions. 5260-1 F 50 - 3

Following this experience the next two incarnations were as females in North Dakota during the pioneer period and the one in 1890.

►Bible Playbook◄

The Law of the LORD Is Perfect...
In the experience [in Persia] the entity gained for it applied the tenets and teachings of the law of one. For the law is perfect, it converteth the soul. [Psa. 19:7]. 5260-1

To Know To Do Good And Not To Do It, Is Sin
To know to do good and not to do it, is sin [Jas. 4:17]. Thus, we find there are periods of sojourns in the earth when individuals would do good, but evil is present with many. 5260-1

As You do Unto the Least of Your Brethren...
As indicated then, we would magnify virtues, we would minimize the faults. For the very fact that the entity has the consciousness, the awareness of self and of its relationships with the Creative Force, and the manifestations of same towards the Maker is evidence that as ye do unto the least of thy brethren, ye do it unto thy Maker [Mat. 25:40]. 5260-1

With What Measure You Mete...
As an individual who would meet or consult, as one who would hire or prepare people, individuals, for their work in large organizations, or as the head of employment bureau, or head of one who would select help. As an individual, the entity is a good judge, then, of human nature, much more than may be implied from the lists of questions the entity oft may ask individuals. For there are the intuitions, and the entity unbeknown to others invites confidences, but remember in thy judgment of others, "As ye do it unto others, ye do it to thy Maker." And with what measurement ye mete, with what judgment ye pass, so may it be done unto thee [Mat. 7:2, Mat. 25:40, Mk. 4:24, Luke 6:38]. 5260-1

Whatsoever A Man Sows...
For the law is not mocked, and whatsoever an individual entity sows, so must it reap [Gal. 6:7]. 5260-1

Answer to her question of how one could develop a larger life, wider outlook and a less selfish, self-centered existence, was: "by applying the words of truth."

Study to Show Thyself Approved
Study to show thyself approved unto God, a workman not ashamed, rightly dividing, divining and applying the words of life [2Tim.2:15] and keeping self unspotted from the world. 5260-1

▶ Needs to Protect Own Sex, As Well As Others
Female Twice to Male to Female Twice

As ye would be protected by others, so protect those of thine own sex, as well as others. 5337-1

A female beauty parlor operator, born in Wisconsin, 11/01/1903, who had incarnated as a female in Egypt during the Ra-Ta period and again in Egypt prior to the Exodus, was a male in Palestine during the period of expectancy of The Messiah when the Romans overran the land, before returning as females again during the gold rush and in Wisconsin.

Leonax [Male] - Customs officer (sort of) Made peace between Romans and Syro-Phoenicians, made it possible for Romans to get together with Hebrews, Syrians, and Samaritans - 5337-1 F 40-3

◀ Bible Playbook ▶

Study to Show Thyself Approved
As first indicated, study to show thyself approved unto thy ideal [2Tim.2:15]. Thus, then, find thy ideal first by analyzing of self, not merely in mind, but do make note of same, erase and add to it as ye analyze thine own body. What are the needs of same and what would be the ideal relationships with others in respect to same? What is the ideal of the mind and its relationships to things, spiritual, things material, things physical, or peoples. Then, what is thy spiritual ideal? 5337-1

As Ye Would Be Forgiven, So Forgive

The entity in the present is oft made the "go-between," one to whom others come for counsel, entrust some of their secrets, as well as some of what is not always "pretty chatter" but the little "catty" things about others. These the entity shouldn't magnify but minimize. For as ye would be forgiven, so forgive [Luke 6:37]. 5337-1

Answer to her query about creating harmony with her mother-in-law, which had karmic implications that can apply to all, was from Proverbs and Romans:

The lack of the harmony may be overcome. This depends, for you are meeting your own self. Better make harmony and you'll make more peace in the home when changes come about. Not burdening of self, but be so kind, be so gentle, be so patient, that ye will heap coals of fire on her head. [Prov. 25:21-22, Rom. 12:20] Ye can, ye know well." 5337-1

▶ Experience Gave Male Ability in Thought
Female to Female to Male to Female Twice

The entity was a man, or of the opposite sex, in that experience, and this causes much of the distress, as well as the ability to become most of the man in its thought and in its expression with others. 5276-1

A female born in London, England, 09/15/1887 that appeared as a female in Egypt during the Exodus, and again in Somerset, England with the daughters of Hezekiah, changed sex and appeared as a male in Palestine when The Master walked in the earth:

Mathias [Male] - Among groups chosen to go on many missions with Jesus, saw and experienced elements obey

His voice [Mat. 8:27, Mk. 4:41, Luke 8:25] - 5276-1 F 56-3

►Bible Playbook◄

Who Will Descend from Heaven...
So the entity, as in Moses, finds itself slow in making comprehension; until he had been through those experiences of even being in the presence of the divine, having given to man the outline of the law, and of how man in his relationship to God, in His relationship to his fellow man, in his relationship to himself could say, as must the entity learn, "Say not who will descend from heaven to bring a message, for lo: the whole law is expressed, is manifested, is indicated within one's own consciousness" [Deut. 30:12]. 5276-1

The Body Is the Temple of the Living God
For the body is indeed the temple of the living God [1 Cor. 6:19] and He hath promised to meet thee there. 5276-1

Prayer - Others, Lord, Others
Here am I, O Lord, use me, send me! And may I seek only to do, to be a channel through which thy blessings, thy promises, may be fulfilled to my friends, my neighbors, those about me. Others, Lord, others! 5276-1

Of Myself I Can Do Nothing...
Condemn not thyself for any fault that may have been in others, or for thy having made choices that have apparently brought outer appearances of activities in others not good. Did the Master condemn self for the ways among men? rather, "Of myself I can do nothing, only as the spirit of truth and of the Father may work in and through me, may I become one with His purposes with me " [John 5:19, John 5:30]. 5276-1

In Him We Live
And He, my friend, is the pattern. He is thy brother, He is

thy Lord. In Him ye live and move and have thy being
[Acts 17:28]. 5276-1

Seek First the Kingdom of Heaven
So, in the present, as the entity seeks may it give in its
writings, in its communications and teachings, the more
important things, or as indicated in the admonitions which
were received by Martha when there were the choosing by
Mary of the more important things. For, as has been
indicated, seeking first the kingdom of heaven, then may all
these things of the material world be added unto thee [Mat.
6:33, 7:7, Luke 11:9]. 5276-1

The Father Knows What You Have Need Of
For He, thy Father-God, knoweth what ye have need of
even before ye ask Him [Mat. 6:8]. 5276-1

Knock and It Is Opened Unto You
Ask and ye shall find Him, knock and it is opened unto thee
[Mat. 7:7, Luke 11:9]. 5276-1

Behold, I Stand At the Door and Knock
Even as He knocks at thy heart may ye hear and open, that
He may enter [Rev. 3:20]. 5276-1

Love The Lord With All Thy Heart...
Love the Lord with all thine heart and mind and soul and
thy neighbor as thyself [Mat. 22:37-39]. 5276-1

Answer to the question about her feeling of responsibility
for her sister committing suicide, and whether returning to
England would have prevented it was:

Let the Dead Past Bury Its Dead
Not responsible, but these are condemnations, as has been
indicated, arising from experiences in the earth; but leave
them where they belong. Let the dead past bury its dead

[Mat. 8:22, Luke 9:60]. 5276-1

► **Gentleness and Patience from Male Experience**
Female to Female to Male to Female Twice

Hence the gentleness and the ability to aid much through the patience of the entity in the present; though the entity would declare that it was very short at times. These arise from the abilities through that sojourn as the man. 3042-1

A female chiropractor born in Walton, Delaware Co., New York, 01/17/1880, who had been females in Atlantis during the first upheaval and in the household of the king in Persia during the Uhjltd period, was male during the Norse Voyages to early New York during the first attempts at settling in the new land where he gained by being security for others:

Jonathan Sidewelle - Norse, seaman, "rough and tough," made many excursions in various ports and lands, found short way across New York State "and brought periods of activity that were disappointing in the material but that in the mental and spiritual grew through those periods." 3042-1 F 63 - 3

Following that incarnation, he was female during the Gold Rush and the one in 1880.

Answer to the query of how to make the most of the remaining years was a repeat from 2 Timothy given earlier:

◄**Bible Playbook**►

Study to Show Thyself Approved Unto God
Then study to show thyself approved unto God, a workman not ashamed, but rightly dividing the words of truth [2 Tim. 2:15], putting the emphasis upon that which is needed;

keeping self from condemnation [Jas. 1:27]. 3042-1

As Ye Mete To Others...
For, as ye mete to others it is measured to thee again [Mat. 7:2, Mk. 4:24, Luke 6:38]. 3042-1

Her query whether she should continue to study with the Rosicrucian Order, (A.M.O.R.C.) which she has been doing for 18 years or some other group was:

Study Deuteronomy 30
Self is quite different and quite better! For, when ye know self ye know the rest of the universe. This may be well to use as a judgment. There is no better book than the 30th Deuteronomy! 3042-1

▶ Gained Mind of a Business Man
Female Four Times to Male to Female Twice

Thus we find those principles because of which the entity has at times been termed, "You have the mind of a business man." These are innate and manifested, dependent upon the abilities of the entity to coordinate circumstance with its ideals in every phase of relationship. 2560-1

A female 65 born in Detroit, Michigan, 10/19/1875, who had been females in Atlantis prior to first breakup, in Egypt during the Ra-Ta period, in Persia during the Uhjltd period and in Rome when the church was being formed in Laodicea, was next a male in the Norse land when there was the breaking up of tradition and entering Hun land and eastern France.

Doloros Olin [Male] Leader/ruler, directed affairs of peoples, and principles under which various groups and states of activity were formulated, "gained when there was the expression of the universal consciousness or for the good of all; lost when there was the selfish or personal gain expressed in some of the activities." - 2560-1 F 65- 5

Following that life as a male, he incarnated as females in Early Ft. Dearborn and the one in 1875.

Innate Abilities

Again we see those principles innate in the present experience of the entity; its abilities to pass judgments upon or to draw upon rules of order and the regulating influences in the experiences of groups to which the entity may belong or in which it may be associated or affiliated. 2560-1

►Bible Playbook◄

You Do Not Gather Figs from Thistles

For, as in the material world ye find that ye do not gather figs from thistles, [Mat. 7:16] neither in the mental world may one think hate and find love in one's bosom; neither in the spiritual realm may one entertain the desire for ego to express irrespective of others and find the beauty of the spiritual thinking life. 2560-1

With What Measure You Mete…

Study well, then, the influence ye have upon those ye meet day by day. For, again, with what measure ye mete, with what judgment ye act, so comes it back to thee [Mat. 7:2, Mk. 4:24, Luke 6:38]. For, to have love one must manifest and show love in one's life and one's dealings with others. To have friends one must show self friendly. 2560-1

If Ye Will Be My Children, I Will Be Your God

In the present experience, practice much of that ye attained and gained there; [in Rome] and ye will find that there will shine more and more into thy experience that feeling of the closeness, the oneness of that promise, "If ye will be my children, I will be your God." [Lev. 26:12, Jer. 7:23; 11:4; 30:22; Ezek. 36:28] These words are personal, as ye experience, as ye know. They are promises that bring to remembrance the beauties, the joys of welldoing; not so much the material things but that as may not be bought with a price save the WILL to be a manifestation and an expression of that creative influence ye call God. 2560-1

Pearls of Great Price
For, the entity learned that the pearls of great price are not merely those activities from the affliction of a mollusk in the sea as it resists; but that as ye in thy experience resist that as would lead to selfish desires, the gratifying of selfish motives, ye build the pearls of great price [Mat. 13:46]. 2560-1

As Ye Would That Men Should Do To You...
Hence [from Egyptian in Said] we find the interest evinced by the entity in the songs of those of old, as they were and are given as the means in which the problems of individuals in every walk or phase of life have become as lessons in their activities; and how that they come again to that which is the basic principle of the manifestation of spirit in the earth, "As ye would that men should do to you, do ye even so to them" [Mat. 7:12]. 2560-1

Hold Fast To That Which Is Good
Serve the Living God
Fear at times arises as to the outcome of all the turmoil. Yet know, as ye did preach, as ye did practice as the princess of that land [Atlantis] ye must hold fast to that which is good; [1Thes. 5:21] determining that others may do as they may, but as for thee and thy house, ye will serve a LIVING God [Jos. 24:15]. 2560-1

Your Body Is the Temple of the Living God

For, His promise is that in the temple in thy temple He will meet thee, in the holy of holies. And thy body is the temple of the living God. There He will meet thee [1 Cor. 6:19]. 2560-1

He Requires Mercy Not Sacrifice

Let thy light keep bright within thine own purpose. Analyze thy purposes oft; not as to become self-centered, not as to justify anything. For, He requireth not sacrifice at thy hands [Hos. 6:6, Mat. 12:7, Mat. 9:13] but that ye GLORIFY Him before others. 2560-1

►Now Men Stop to Listen when she Speaks
Female to Female to Male to Female Twice

A female born in Coin, Iowa, 04/13/1885 who had been a female in the Egyptian Ra-Ta period, in the Persian Uhjltd period and in Europe during the Roman Expansion, was a male in England during the Crusades:

Cowpers [Male] Organized groups under Bruce. 2029-1 F 54-4

Abilities

From that experience the entity gains the abilities to be a counselor to not only those of its own sex but to those of the opposite sex. And when the entity speaks, most men stop to listen, and do not consider "just a woman speaking," This can be said of very few women. 2029-1

Following the experience as a crusader, he returned as a female in Salem during the period of the witchcraft trials and again in the one in 1885.

Influences/Urges

In each of those that influences the entity in the present,

then, we find such being more often the promptings of the inmost self. 2029-1

As is understood by the entity, then, that to which it may attain is only limited by the desire of the heart, and the purposes for which it would give its service. 2029-1

◀Bible Playbook▶

In Him Ye Live and Move and Have Thy Being
For in Him ye live and move and have thy being indeed [Acts 17:28]. And as ye do it to the least of thy brethren, ye do it to thy Maker [Mat. 25:40, 45]. 2029-1

The Giver of All Good and Perfect Gifts
Then, study; analyze self and the desire and the purposes. See if these are in keeping with thy ideal, that was, that is set in Him, the Giver of all good and perfect gifts [Jas. 1:17]. 2029-1

Answer to the query where she could get concrete guidance besides from the inner voice was:

Don't Climb Up another Way
Seek not other than that of His meeting thee within thine own temple [1 Cor. 6:19]. For beside Him there is none other. Know, as He gave, they that climb up some other way are robbers [John 10:1]. 2029-1

▶Innate Urge: Male Abilities
Female to Female to Male to Female Twice

Hence those latent and innate urges for the capacities for man's work, for man's abilities, arise from those experiences or sojourns. These are good if used properly. 189-3

A female secretary born in Brooklyn, New York, 07/04/1894, who had been a female in the Ra-Ta period in Egypt, a female in the Holy Land during the Return from Captivity where she had been given a male name, Hannahar, because of her abilities to compete, to cope with the best of the male workers, was next a male in England during the Crusades to Holy Land:

Edmond Blachard [Male] - Crusader, looked for power through an idea set as a criterion rather than teachings that prompted same, gained materially, but lost spiritually and mentally by tendency to dominate by force - 0189-3 F 42-3

Following the experience as a Crusader, he incarnated as a female during the American Revolution, another period of conflict in which she suffered physically and mentally, before the one in 1894.

►Bible Playbook◄

All Must Pass Under the Rod
For all must pass under the rod [Ezek. 20:37], or under the experiences of every form of activity in a material world as to place, position, sex, and the abilities for the use or application of material gains. 189-3

Cast Your Bread upon the Waters
Then we find that the earthly sojourns become the emotional forces that oft in the experience of this entity have produced, or have proven to be, those experiences where the little hurts have come from the indifference of those whom the entity has in its goodness of grace aided. Hence these have brought discouragements and wonderments at times. But there should ever be the knowledge in the experience of the entity that bread cast upon the waters will return in due season [Eccl. 11:1], and

that to be in a material world a light of goodness - as is exemplified in the hope of the eternal and the divine that is innate in the experience of every soul - becomes the growth in the soul development in material sojourns. 189-3

What Ye Sow, Ye Reap –
With What Measure Ye Mete...

For in the experiences or sojourns an entity is constantly meeting itself. For what ye sow, so do ye reap - or that indeed ye reap; and with what measure ye mete it is measured to you again [Mat. 7:2, Mk. 4:24, Luke 6:38, Gal. 6:7]. 189-3

Each Soul is His Brother's Keeper

But all power, all force, arises from one source; and those that have same are only lended same by an All-Wise and Merciful Creator as talents to be used in His vineyard.189-3 For each entity, each soul, IS his brother's keeper! [Gen. 4:9] 189-3

The LORD Our God Is One LORD

For as the Lord thy God is ONE [Deut. 6:4, Mk. 12:29], so is the law under which, through which, one attains fellowship as one with Him. 189-3

The Word Is Already In Your Own Heart

Look not for those who may bring a message from abroad, or those who may descend from the heavens to bring word again, but rather into thine own heart [Deut. 30:11-14]. For THERE He hath promised to meet all. 189-3

Study to Show Thyself Approved Unto God

As to the abilities of the entity in the present, then, and that to which it may attain, and how:

First, study to show thyself approved unto God, a workman not ashamed, rightly divining - or dividing - the words of truth; [2Tim.2:15] that is, giving proper evaluations to the material, the mental and the spiritual relationships, the economic, the social, the orders of things in their proper form. 189-3

If God Be For Us, Who Can Be Against Us

For they that be upon the Lord's side have nothing to fear [Rom. 8:31], and have charm, personality, life, living as an ever effervescing, as an ever bubbling over in the experience with others. 189-3

Keep Self Unspotted From the World
God Loves the Cheerful Giver

Keep self unspotted from the world [Jas. 1:27] of thine own consciousness, condemning none - and most of all not self. God loveth the cheerful giver [2 Cor. 9:7]. 189-3

Answer to her query of how to broaden her intellect, repeated the advice previously given and expanded it:

Not the Letter of the Law, But the Spirit

As given, by studying to show thyself approved [2Tim.2:15] unto the LAW thou hast set, or aided in setting, for many; in the interpretation of same. Not as law and the letter of same, rather - as has been indicated - in the application of the SPIRIT of same [2 Cor. 3:6].

►Inhibits Associations of a Conjugal Nature
Female to Female Twice to Male to Female

…while there is the desire for home and home life, we find that those experiences as Jean Juahn Destuyvelent made for those activities that have prevented the entity in the present from making associations of a conjugal nature. - 3027-2 F 37-4

A female stenographer born in Mons En Bardeuil-Le Lille, France, 09/15/1908, who had been females in Atlantis, where she had been of the Law of One but listening to others rejected Him, who is the way, in Egypt during the Ra-Ta period, and in Palestine when The Master walked in the earth was male in America during the Revolution:

Jean Juahn DeStuyvelent [Male] - General, not in name but abilities, close to LaFayette, came into land with soldiers, brought favors to efforts of LaFayette and Washington from associations with those in authority and politics - 3027-2 F 37-4

◄Bible Playbook►

Choose You This Day Whom You Will Serve
Thus, as in most entities, this experience will be either one in which the entity will succeed or make a complete failure. Whether this is mental, material or spiritual depends upon the choices made by the entity. Not that one may not excel in all, yet - as given of old - many are called but few respond. There is ever before an individual entity life and death, good and evil. The entity is given the ability to choose [Deut. 30:15, Jos. 24:15]. 3027-2

Think Not More Highly of Self...
He Who Will Be the Greatest...
These activities enable the entity in the present to carry weight when many another will fail, whatever the attempts may be in a political sense, whether socially or in politics alone. But remember, think not more highly of self than ye ought to think [Rom. 12:3]. And he or she that is the greatest among the fellows, among the associates, is the one who may serve the better [Mat. 20:27, Mat. 23:11, Mk. 10:44]. 3027-2

Study to Show Thyself Approved

As to the abilities of the entity in the present, that to which it may attain, and how: First, know thyself and thy ideal, - spiritually, mentally, materially.

Then study to show thyself approved [2Tim.2:15] unto that ideal, and know ye chose wisely in Laodicea. Know that He is the way, has ever been the way; just as ye rejected Him in the Atlantean experiences, through the voices as were heard, and yet ye may again arouse this to that activity. But wait ye on the Lord, show thyself approved, a workman not ashamed. 3027-2

Answer to the queries if she has made any progress in the last two or three incarnations and what progress or retrogression has she made during this present life had a biblical overtone:

Judge Not, That Ye Be Not Judged

There is progress whether ye are going forward or backward! The thing is to move!

No one may be the judge of that ye have chosen [Mat. 7:1-2, Luke 6:37]. Do RIGHT! 3027-2

▶ Sees Most any Proposition from Male Viewpoint
Female to Female Three Times to Male to Female

The entity is one very intuitive, irrespective of what it may do or has done about same; with quite an ability as a leader or director in whatever undertaking is begun. For innately the entity sees most any proposition from the viewpoint of a man, for of course it was a man in the appearance before this. 0371-2

A female born in Dayton, Ohio, 10/01/1898, who had been an Egyptian/Persian in Egypt during the Ra-Ta period, the granddaughter of the King of Judah in Assyria during the Captivity of Jews by Assyrians, and a female Viking in England at the time of early expansion, was a male indigenous American Medicine Man at the time of early settlers the Ohio area:

Medicine Man [Male] - Indigenous American, "with the abilities to direct, the abilities to use nature's activities for the controlling of and the directing of the activities of many of its peoples." 0371-2 F 40 - 4

►Bible Playbook◄

As You Treat Your Fellow Man...
As to the abilities of the entity in the present, and that to which it may attain, and how:

First, as to how; know that, as ye have experienced through thy material sojourns, each entity has its job, as well as its privilege, its opportunity, and these are to be used purposefully and not for a selfish motive but in those directions as may be in the glorifying of that cause or purpose or creative force for which, for the indwelling with which, each is preparing self.

Thus in the manner as ye treat thy fellow man, so ye do to thy Maker [Mat. 25:40]. 371-2

Study Then To Show Thyself Approved
Study then to show thyself approved unto thy Maker, a workman not ashamed; but rightly EVALUING the experiences, and His promises in thy association with thy fellow man [2Tim.2:15].

►Found Much More in Women than Before
Female to Female Twice to Male to Female

A female Stenographer born in Paterson, New Jersey in 1907, who had been females in Atlantis, in Egypt during the Ra-Ta period and in Persia during the Uhjltd period, was next a male in France during the Crusades before returning as a female

Marcelus Dewetherna [Male] Crusader, found just as good individuals among those he thought were heathen or that had forgotten God, finding that their approach was a little different through one who was as a brother to his Lord, became confused, determined in self never to be a man again, found much more in women than he had trusted in them before. -3376-2 F 36 – 4

◀Bible Playbook▶

The Lord thy God is one
The Lord thy God is one [Deut. 6:4, Mk. 12:29]. The self as an individual entity, body, mind and soul is one. The soul is a child of God, or a thought, a corpuscle in the heart of God. Yet the entity, thine own soul, has been given a will to use the attributes of soul, mind and body to thine own purposes. Thus as the individual entity applies self in relationship to those facts, the entity shows itself to be a true child or a wayward child, or a rebellious child, of the Creative Force or God. 3376-2

Thou Shall Love the Lord Thy God
Then it would behoove the entity to first study what is the law of the Lord thy God. It is bound up in the admonition that thou shalt love the Lord with all thy mind, thy heart and thy soul, and thy neighbor as thyself [Mat. 22:37-39, Mk. 12:30-31, Luke 10:27]. 3345-1

As You Sow, So Shall You Reap
The laws pertaining to same are ever true that the manner

in which ye treat thy fellow man ye are treating thy Maker. The seed ye sow ye shall also reap [Gal. 6:7]. 3345-1

Three Highly Unusual Sex Change Entries:

Other entries in the *Who Was Who* sex change category that stand out include that of a female pilot whose vocational abilities crossed genders, a beauty parlor operator, whose sex changes spanned two critical periods, and a married couple who were in the same periods, but in reverse genders:

▶ Pattern of Vocational Abilities Crossing Genders
Female to Female to Male to Female Twice

A female Pilot born in New York, New York, 04/15/1913, who was discriminated against because of her gender most of the time, yet became the first female Executive Pilot and flew for a corporation and started her own company delivering airplanes to foreign countries in 1965 had been a female Atlantean in Egypt during the Ra-Ta period, who controlled communications with other lands and flying boats, a female Grecian emissary, sent to undermine, in Persia during the Uhjltd period where she established communications and brought development for steering ships and installation of compass in means of communication, was next a male in Rome during the period of expansion of Empire:

Gialdo [Male] - In diplomatic service, planned manner and means of communications with other lands - 3184-1 F 30-3

After that life, where she combined her abilities from her previous lives, she incarnated as females in Early America after reconstruction following the Revolutionary war, where her diplomatic abilities manifested as a Secret

Messenger. However, she became disappointed, felt efforts were not fully appreciated by those in power. All of those feelings manifested in her life as the female in New York who never married because she found flying more interesting than men.

►Bible Playbook◄

It Is Within Your Own Heart
…For each individual finds the motivative influence of its life within its own self, and that is correct as was stated of old by the lawgiver: Think not as to who will descend from heaven to give a message or who would come from over the sea that ye might learn and understand. For lo it is within thine own heart, thine own mind [Deut. 30:11-14]. 3184-1

Your Body Is the Temple of the Living God
Thy body is indeed the temple of the living God [1 Cor. 6:19]. He has promised to meet thee and, know that all in the mental, all in the material, has its inception, its conception, in spirit, in purpose, in hope, in desire. Know thy relationship, then, first, with that ye hope for. For life (or God), immortality of the soul, is real; as may be seen from thine own urges if ye analyze them correctly. 3184-1

Only Self Can Separate You…
For as indicated there is naught that may separate thee from the knowledge of the eternal save self [Rom. 8:38-39]. If self finds the emotions at times injected in the mental, turn it over look at the other side. For, upon the side Marked END, on the other is Marked GO go do the biddings as may be the prompting of the eternal influences within; and ye will find peace and harmony in thy undertakings. 3184-1

Do Not Do Any Activity to Be Seen of Men
Remember the first principles, do not that in any activity to

be seen of men [Mat. 23:5]; rather with that purpose to be seen of thy Maker. 3184-1

The Law of the Lord Is Perfect
Keep the faith in self and in self's abilities. But let that faith be guided by the divine and not of self or selfish interests. The law of the Lord is perfect [Psa. 19:7]; so may be thy purposes with thy brother. These keep.3184-1

▶Sex Change Spanning Two Critical Periods
Female to Male Twice to Female Twice

A female beauty parlor operator born in Richmond, Virginia, 05/10/1930, who had been the second daughter of Ra-Ta in the Egyptian period, was in a changed sex in Palestine as a Roman spy when The Master walked in the earth and also in England/France as a questionable character during the Crusades

Philoas [Male?] Roman spy, recorder of activities of emissaries, instructors, tax collectors, did not misuse abilities for self-advantage, gained from associations with early Christians. 2572-1 F 11 -2

William Cowan [Male] Known as "Handsome Billy," involved in activities questioned by many, questionable love affair with Margat Ingals [2571Si] did not terminate well. 2572-1 F 11 – 3

Answer to her question concerning what purpose she came to her present parents, which had wide application, was:

At times it may be considered as an opportunity; at others as a test for self as well as for them. 2572-1

Know that ye are meeting thy own self, in the activities

and in the measure of those influences which prompt between the manifesting of self and the manifesting of self to the glory of the Creative Forces. 2572-1

Let that light which has oft guided thee be the promptings through thy activity. Forget not to pray oft. And let thy prayer be oft - but in thy own words: 2572-1

◄Bible Playbook►

Prayer
Lord, here am I! Use me as thou seest fit. Let me be willing, O God, to be that thou would have me be; that I may bring glory to the Son - who is the Way [John 14:6] for all. 2572-1

►Dual Reverse Sex Changes
Female to Male to Female Twice
Male to Female to Male Three Times

The most interesting sex changes in Greece during the period when emphasis was on the body beautiful and the stage were those of a married couple who appeared in reverse genders:

A female Oral Hygienist born in Detroit, Michigan, 04/03/1914 that had incarnated as a female in ancient Egypt during the Ra-Ta period when individuals were being prepared for motherhood, next appeared as a male in Greece before returning to the female gender.

Her husband, an Osteopath born in Kirksville, Missouri, 06/30/1907, who had been a male Atlantean hospital assistant in Egypt during the Ra-Ta period, entered as a female in Greece before returning to the male gender:

Herecelecon [Male] - Modeled in clay and stone, later introduced games, such as handball, to Roman land 1074-2 F 27- 2

Zeeun [Female] assisted others preparing for conception by injecting into the thoughts, minds, and experiences the need for care of channel through which souls and bodies would be brought into materiality. 1885-2 M 32 - 2

Following this experience as a female, the husband incarnated as a Norse male twice with similar names. He was Bucuos Odel in Alsace, where he supplied remedies for healing from the soil and vegetation and Beucus Olmson in Early Ft. Dearborn, where they were reunited when she was Maya:

Maya - Indigenous American, excelled in woodcraft and games, wife of Beucus Olmson [1885Hu], a Norse trader who treated her badly at times 1074-2 F 27-3

◄Bible Playbook for the Husband◄

There Is A Way Which Seems Right unto Man...
...Do not confuse spiritually with emotions that haven't spiritual background or spiritual ending. Know there are times, as oft in thine own experience, when a way seemeth right unto a man (physical), but the end thereof is death [Prov. 14:12, 16:25]. 1885-2

Know the Author of Your Faith
Know thy ideals, and that these must be founded upon spiritual concepts. Know the author of thy faith; not only by words but by that such has brought, does bring, into thy experience. Know as to the ability of the author of thy faith [2Tim.1:12], and hope, to keep that ye may commit unto it through any experience. 1885-2

Part III
Sex Changes Through the Ages

Eras in the *Who Was Who* where sex changes occurred include the Ancient Egypt Ra-Ta Period, Old Testament Periods of the Exodus and the Return from Captivity. the Greek Classical Period, the Greco-Roman Period, the Roman Periods of Expansion of Empire and of Augustus Caesar, the Early Christian Era, the Pre-Columbian Norse Voyages, the Crusades, Journeys to the New World, the English Restoration, the Early America Settlings, the Salem Witch Trials, and the American and French Revolutionary periods.

►14 ◄
Ancient Egypt

One of the destinations of the five-point projection of consciousness out of Eden symbolized as the Nile River was KMT: "Land of the Black" later known as Egypt, which represented the sense of taste. (Sub-Sahara Africa was under water at that time.)

A period widely covered in the Cayce files is the pre-historic Ra-Ta period in Egypt 10,300 B.C. In that period, the land, which was fertile, was invaded by a group from the sight projection, who saw what they had, wanted it and took it by invasion.

1. Ra-Ta Period
Male to Female, to Female Twice

A female born in Hopkinsville, Kentucky, 12/14/1861, who had been a male ruler in Peru during the period of the Ohums [Ayramas?], was in a changed sex in the next incarnation in Ancient Egypt during the second rule of the Ra-Ta period:

> **Queen Isisis** - Wife of invading ruler, Arart [165], submerged by son, Araaraart [341Gs], became enraged, attempted to assume control of affairs, lived many years after son ascended to kingship. - 0265-1 (2) F 63 -2

Following that incarnation she returned as females in Rome, when the first laws were being given, in England as Queen Henrietta Marie - Daughter of Henry IV of France, wife of Charles I of England, and the one in 1861.

Advice on how to remedy the condition of dissatisfaction and bring the best conditions to her and others was:

►Bible Playbook◄

Study to show self approved unto Him
Study to show self approved unto Him [2Tim.2:15], who is the giver of all good and perfect gifts [Jas. 1:17], through finding the oneness in Him. 265-1

2. Ra-Ta Period
Male to Female Three Times

A female born in Staten Island, NY 10/15/1883 had been a male Emissary in the Ra-Ta Period in Egypt:

> **Lei-Diie [Male]** Emissary, first to establish worship of the Most High in what is now the Grecian land experienced much turmoil under the various strains and rules.1742-2 F 47 - 1

After that life of turmoil, he returned as females in Rome during the Early Christian era and to France, when Alsace was being overrun by others, and the one in 1883.

◄Bible Playbook►

Give Unto Others…
Give out; even as ye have received, give unto others [Mat. 10:8]. 1742-2

Line upon Line, Precept upon Precept
In helping, in giving out to others may the unfoldment come; not in those things that would become as evil SPOKEN of [Rom. 14:15], but in little acts of kindness, little words here and there for little by little, line upon line, precept upon precept [Isa. 28:10, 13], does one gain in self, and add to others. 1742-2

►15◄
Old Testament

1. Exodus
Female to Male to Female Twice

A female born in Youngstown, Ohio, 10/30/1904 went from an incarnation as a princess of the Law of One in Atlantis to an Israelite in a changed sex in the wilderness during the Exodus:

Barthuel [Male] Among the sons of the children of Israel endowed with abilities to prepare the Ark of the Covenant, especially in overlay work with metal and wood, very active, but very quiet. 1747-3 F 34 - 2

After that life during the Exodus, he returned to the Holy Land in a changed sex as a relative of Mary, Martha and Lazarus in Palestine and experienced the tremors of Golgotha following the crucifixion before the one in 1904.

▶Bible Playbook◀

I AM the Resurrection and the Life
I AM the resurrection, the life. [John 11:25] I TOLD thee to destroy the body and in three days I would raise it again [Mat. 27:63, Mk. 8:31]. This must become a fact. Then it is understood how the emblem represents God, the way, the cross, self, the world, as to how there is the activity through same. 1747-3

In the expressions of self in the present, then, have more activity, more appreciation of the body because of its being the temple of the soul [1 Cor. 6:19] and BEING a channel through which the awarenesses of the other influences may be felt the world, the flesh and the spirit, as well as evil. And as these are applied in the experience of the entity, we find there may be the greater and greater understanding, the greater abilities for the relationships becoming more worthwhile. 1747-3

2. Exodus
Female to Male to Female Four Times

A female born in Brockton, Massachusetts, 12/01/1917, who had been a female in Temple service in ancient Egypt during the Ra-Ta period, returned in a changed sex during the Exodus:

Shemelack [Male] Helped prepare skins, linens, and rings for tabernacle 1771-2 F 21 --2

Following that incarnation, he returned in a changed sex in Persia as niece of the Queen during the time of activity under the line of Croesus where she used prompting from the male work experience, in Rome during the early Christian Period and twice in Massachusetts: during the settlings in Early America and the one in 1917.

►Bible Playbook◄

Nothing Can Separate You from the Love of God
As to the abilities of the entity in the present, then, and that to which it may attain, and how: This is limited only to self. For be persuaded, there is nothing in heaven or hell that may prevent thee from knowing thy relationship to thy Creator BUT thyself [Rom. 8:38-39]. 1771-2

Press on to the Mark of the Higher Calling
Laying aside then the things that may easily beset, press on to the mark of the higher callings [Phil. 3:14] that are set in thy abilities to USE thy activities in ANY of the decorative forces. For the beauty of man's mind is oft directed by the beauty of his environs. 1771-2

3. Exodus
Female to Female to Male to Female Twice

A female born in Roselle, New Jersey, 12/14/1916, who had been an Atlantean priestess who escaped to the Incal land during the breakup and a female who compiled formulas for mental and internal exercises of mind to control activities of the body in Ancient Egypt during the Ra-Ta period was in a changed sex during the period of the Exodus preparing incense offering for the holy of holies before entering as a female twice more.

Shuelmeur [Male] Apothecary, worked with herb and oil combinations for special essence and odors applied for preparation of attuning mind from material to spiritual. 3285-2 F 27-3

This appearance was followed by that of a female in England during the Crusades, who had been left behind by her companion and became a sorceress/divinator through her own wits and used charms and magic to attain desires and purposes for material things, and again in 1916.

▶ Bible Playbook ◀

There Is Daily Set before You Good and Evil
For, as has been indicated, when the entity sets itself to do something, it accomplishes it whether good or bad. But make a choice. For there is daily set before thee good and evil, life and death, and with thy choice ye make it good or bad [Deut. 30:15, Jos. 24:15]. 3285-2

The Lord Will Not Withhold Any Good Thing
Not that one should become goody-goody far from it! For know that the Lord will not withhold any good thing [Psa. 84:11] spiritually, mentally or materially from those who love His coming. 3285-2

Your Body Is the Temple of the Living God
How oft, then, do you come to the Lord or through thy prayers have the Lord approach thee? Indeed thy body is the temple of the living God. [1 Cor. 6:19] Keep it beautiful, to be sure, as it is but not to vainglory, nor to such an extent as to forget that for which the body was given thee: That thy soul, which may be a companion with God, might manifest among thy fellow beings. Appreciate it! Glorify it, sure but to God, not to man! 3285-2

1. Return from Captivity
Female to Male to Female Twice

A female born in from Memphis, Tennessee 11/12/1886, went from life as a female in ancient Egypt during the Ra-Ta period to that of a male in the Holy Land with the last group to return from captivity with Nehemiah

Shulemite **[Male]** Benjaminite/Judahite, scribe/ translator, associated with those in temple and the activities of teaching, interpreting, and changing law to language of the day- 1499-1 F 50 - 2

Following that experience, he was a female in early Philadelphia, Pa. at the time when they were seeking religious freedom.

►Bible Playbook◄

The Letter of the Law Kills - the Spirit Gives Life
Hence we will find in the present the entity is a good linguist, one easily able to learn or to interpret other languages. The associations of the entity with peoples of various tongues will be a part of the experience. Yet the letter of the law and the spirit of the law [2 Cor. 3:6] not only of man but of God becomes a reckoning, or an experience or a judgment to be made by the entity in this present experience. 1499-1

The Author and Finisher of Thy Faith
For indeed if these last be the aims, the purposes in self, they must eventually turn upon thee. But if the seeds and the purposes are of truth, and knowledge pertaining to the spiritual associations in the activities these being the cause, the purpose, yea the very author of thy faith, thy confidence, thy desire then we may expect and we may

know these will grow and bring the fruits of the spirit; enabling each soul to become more patient, more longsuffering, more charitable; with stronger fellowships and the abilities to know, though the world may be against thee, though there may be trials and tribulations, there may be even want in body and want in the material things for the body, yet that food which is found in Him as the author and finisher of thy faith [Heb. 12:2] becomes the bread of life, the water of life, the true vine that is, the Son. 1499-1

All Power Has Been Given Into His Keeping
For indeed He is the Creator, He indeed is the Maker of all that doth appear. For all power in heaven and in earth has been given into His keeping [Mat.. 28:18] through the faith He kept with His fellowman; by His advent into the earth, by His doing good in all ways, at all times, under every circumstance. 1499-1

He Has Given His Angels Charge Concerning You
For He hath indeed given His angels charge concerning thee [Mat. 4:6, Luke 4:10, Psa. 91:11]. 1499-1

Try Me
He hath promised indeed, "When ye call I will HEAR and answer speedily." Yea, He hath given, "Try me" [Psa. 139:23]. 1499-1

My Peace I Leave With Thee
...purge thyself of lust of every nature that ye may indeed know that peace as He gave, "My peace I leave with thee; [John 14:27] not as the world counteth peace but as the Lord of love, of grace, of mercy." THESE be that peace that bringeth gladness and joy to the heart to be counted to be worthy to know His love in thy experience day by day. 1499-1

Bless Them Which Despitefully Use You

Yet the entity in the latter portion grew to the ability to forgive even those who had despitefully used [Mat. 5:44, Luke 6:28] the confidences of the self. 1499-1

If The World Hate You, Know That It Hated Me

Yet this lies dormant and yet knows, even as He gave, "Abiding in me for if the world hated me, [John 15:18] it will hate thee also for thy very goodness, for thy mercy, for thy grace," yet ye will have the abiding peace, if ye will abide in same, that will bring forth fruit WORTHY of acceptation by Him who is the Lord and the Judge of the earth. 1499-1

And we find the entity then, though in the opposite sex from the present, was among the scribes and translators of those activities during that experience; and associated with those in the temple as well as in those activities that gave the ministry in the teaching, the interpreting, the changing of the law as befitted the language of the day. 1499-1

Walk Not In the Paths of the Ungodly

Walk not in the paths of the ungodly [Psa. 1:4]; though ye may know, though ye may see even as He the slime and the slum, and those things that make men afraid; yet the souls of these are as dear in the sight of the Father as thy own. And what hath He given as being the whole law? 1499-1

Love The Lord With All Your Heart...

Love the Lord with all thy heart, thy mind, thy body, and thy neighbor as thyself! [Mat. 22:37-39, Mk. 12:30-31, Luke 10:27] 1499-1

As You Do Unto The Least of These...

"For as ye do unto the least of these, my children," saith the Lord, "ye do it unto me!" [Mat. 25:40, 45] 1499-1

Answer to the query if she would find the Way in her current life? Was:

Let Him In
He knocketh at thy door of thy heart. OPEN! Let Him enter! [Rev. 3:20] Study, read not as rote, but see as thou readest that it is to THEE the message comes the 14th, 15th, 16th, 17th of John; and ye will know it is thee that He is speaking to, speaking with. 1499-1

The Truth Shall Make You Free
And ye will know, and the truth will make thee free [John 8:32] of the LAW as law. 1499-1

A Soft Answer Turns Away Wrath
Live day by day in that way and manner that, as He hath given, the soft answer turneth away wrath [Prov. 15:1; Rom. 12:20]. As the gentleness and kindness that ye may give and show in the experience and in the associations make for heaping coals of fire as it were upon his OWN inner self [Prov. 25:22], these will bring out, these will burn out, that which is amiss in his experience. 1499-1

Answer to her query if she would become a charge of the state in her old age was:

Trust in Him
This depends upon the application of self in the present. NO! Not if ye trust in Him who IS the Giver, the Maker of all that is! [Jas. 1:17] 1499-1

2. Return from Captivity
Female to Male to Female Twice

A female born in Norton, Pennsylvania, 11/04/1894, who became a Government Clerk in charge of War Department Photographic Library went from life as a female in ancient

Egypt to the life as a male in the Holy Land time of Ezra and Nehemiah during the return from captivity re-writing and translating law after walls were rebuilt:

Samathana [Male] Son of Meshach, helped translate law preserved from writings of Joshua, Joseph, and Moses, gained ability to translate -2970-1 F 48 - 2

Abilities/Advice
In the present these are manifested in that the entity is a good teacher, a good interpreter for self and yet few interpret the same in the entity that the entity interprets in self! A good reader, a good datastician. These arise from the experience then, as Samathana. 2970-1

Following that life, he returned as females during the early Christian era, the period of the American gold rush and the one in Norton, Pennsylvania.

► Bible Playbook ◄

Your Body is the Temple of the Living God
In this basis, then: Know that thy body, thy mind, thy soul, is a manifestation of God in the earth as is every other soul; and that thy body is indeed the temple of the living God [1 Cor. 6:19]. All the good, then, all the God, then, that ye may know, is manifested in and through thyself and not what somebody else thinks, not what somebody else does! For, that is a nice way of the devil in his workshop "Do because somebody else does! Think of that because somebody else does!" 2970-1

The Lord thy God is ONE as thou art one [Deut. 6:4, Mk. 12:29]. 2970-1

I Will Never Leave You

Then, be one in thy purpose. Know, as given of old, the man called Jesus is the Savior of the world. He has purchased with His own will that right for direction. And He has promised, "I will never leave thee [Mat. 28:20, John 14:18] I will not forsake thee," save that THOU as an individual cast Him out, or reject Him, for counsel from some other source. 2970-1

Don't Hide Your Light under a Bushel

It is true that the home is as some other place to thee, save as it is the desire of thy companion and of thyself to be like others and have a home. These are urges, just as the analyzing of self, not listening to the voices without. For, know that His promise is that He will meet thee within thine own temple [1 Cor. 6:19], not in John Henry or in James Monroe, or in anyone else's but thine own! 2970-1

Base thy analysis and thy purposes, then, on that declared in the 30th of Deuteronomy, and as promised by Him in the 14th, 15th, 16th and 17th of John. And ye will become positive; ye will become a light for others. For you do not light a candle and put it under a bushel [John 14:18, Mat. 5:15, Mk. 4:21, Luke 11:33]. You do not learn of Him and keep it closed in a book, in a picture, in a song, but ye live His life, ye live His purpose. Thus ye become the witness for Him day by day. 2970-1

He is The Way the Truth and the Life

Would you eliminate thy life, thy hope? Then, reject not Him who is the way and the truth and the life, and has been and is the only way [John 14:6]. 2970-1

Don't Climb Up another Way

They that climb up some other way are thieves and robbers [John 10:1] of their own selves, and their own opportunities. For He ALONE can give peace in thy consciousness. For He is the Prince of Peace, the maker of peace, the builder of peace in the hearts of those that seek His ways. 2970-1

The Earth Is the Lord's and the Fullness Thereof
There's no security in worldly possessions. For the earth is the Lord's and the fullness thereof [Psa. 24:1, 1 Cor. 10:26, 28], and the silver and the gold. [Hag. 2:8] If ye use same for self-indulgence or self-gratification ONLY, ye do so to thine own undoing. And ye are not alone this is man's failing, and the devil's way of handling man. For it brings glory to his own ego to possess, or to be looked up to. 2970-1

He That Is the Greatest Among You...
Forget not, "He that is the greatest among you is the servant of all" [Mat. 20:27, Mat. 23:11, Mk. 10:44]. 2970-1

►16◄
Greek Classical Period

1. Xenophon
Female to Female to Male to Female Twice

A Catholic [Countess?] born in Tegerensee, Bavaria, 07/31/1879, who had been a female active in temple service in Egypt during the Ra-Ta period and a female Indian teacher in Persia during the Uhjltd period, was a male in Greece at time of turmoils when Xenophon was leader in the eastern land before returning as a female:

Grecian? [Male] Close to leader, classified activities of leaders of armies. 2331-1 F 61 - 3

Influences/Urges
Thus in the present, as an organizer in whatever field of service the entity may choose, the entity may find helpful

influences and urges in the experience. Thus the entity is a natural leader, though as indicated at times questioned as to its determining factors. 2331-1

Following that incarnation, he was females in Bavaria when groups were journeying to new lands because of religious persecutions and again in 1879.

►Bible Playbook◄

Study to Show Yourself Approved
Keep Self Unspotted from the World
Study to show thyself approved truth [2Tim.2:15] unto that ideal, in that sincerity ye demand of self and of others; keeping self unspotted [Jas.1:27] from condemnation or question. 2331-1

He Will Not Leave You Comfortless
For, He leaves not those comfortless [John 14:18] who seek to know His way. 2331-1

Seek and You Shall Find...
SEEK and ye shall find; KNOCK and it shall be opened unto thee [Mat. 7:7, Luke 11:9]. 2331-1

The Lord Keeps His Promises
For the Lord keepeth His promises to those who love His coming [1Thes.2:19]. 2331-1

Grow In Grace
Then each entity as this should accept the opportunities, the obligations, the duties, yes, make the duties privileges; that the entity may fill that purpose and thus find self growing in grace [2 Pet. 3:18], in knowledge and in understanding. 2331-1

With What Measure You Mete...

In giving those influences which have been and are as urges latent and manifested in this experience, we find that the sojourns in the environs about the earth[7] are as latent in the dreams, the visions, the real inner self; and thus have their part in the entity making its choices as to its activity, its relationships to others.

For, it is with what measure ye mete to thy fellow men day by day that ye mete to thy better self, thy Maker. For with what measure ye mete, it is measured to thee again [Mat. 7:2, Mk. 4:24, Luke 6:38]. 2331-1

2. Xenophon
Female to Female to Male to Female Twice

A female artist born in Livingston, Alabama, 01/18/1906, who had been an Atlantean high priestess in Egypt during Ra-Ta period and a daughter of Zerubbabel in the Holy Land during the return from captivity, was a male associate of Xenophon in Greece when he sought to override western Asia:

Xerxon [Male] Associate of Xenophon [2903], helper to activities of Grecians 2545-1 F 35 -3

Following the male incarnation he returned as females in Alabama: as Rene Ney, a French princess, in early Alabama and the one in 1906.

► Bible Playbook ◄

Quite Yourself As Such
Then in thy own consciousness, ye are indeed a child of the King. Thou ART a helpmeet in the creation of the earth, the world, the thought of same. As a child of the living God, then, quit thyself as such; [1 Sam.4:9, 1 Cor. 16:13]

knowing that upon His power, His love, His promise ye can put thy trust. For His promise is, "Though ye may be far afield, though ye may be discouraged, though ye may be troubled, if ye call I will hear and answer speedily." 2545-1

God Is Not Mocked

Do not become discouraged. God is not mocked [Gal. 6:7]. These have been testings for thee. For, there are those purposes in thy activities and in thy abilities to DO WHATEVER YE CHOOSE TO DO, whether in teaching, in writing, in bringing to others the understanding of and the appreciation of the beautiful that is a part of thyself; whether in thy music, in thy associations of activities, or in whatever may be thy choice. 2545-1

He That Is Greatest Among You...

For, he that is greatest among you, said He (who knowest all), is the servant of all [Mat. 20:27, Mat. 23:11, Mk. 10:44]. 2545-1

Answer to the query of how to externalize her deep spiritual urges better, or bring them to the conscious mind, was:

Little By Little, Line Upon Line...

It is with patience. ... It is little by little, line upon line, here a little, there a little [Isa. 28:10, Isa. 28:13]. Give expression each day, in each association, in each activity, in such a way that ye bring hope, faith, the SEEKING of the better in self that is in others. This is done by the smile, the cheery word, the better expression of minimizing the faults and magnifying the virtues in all. 2545-1

For, it behooves none of us to speak unkindly of the worst of us, no matter how little, mean or unthoughted. 2545-1

For, the good the image of the Maker is there. 2545-1

Let Thy Light So Shine
Let thy light so shine [Mat. 5:16], day by day, that ye fail
not in that standard thou hast set to thyself. 2545-1

Do not expect others to measure all at once. For, thou art
high indeed in thy ideals. Do not lessen them, but let thy
prayer be daily:

Prayer
Lord, here am I thy servant, seeking to be a greater
expression of thee among my fellow men. Show me the
way, O Lord. Help me to be humble, yet glorify thee.
2545-1

►17◄
Greco/Roman Period

1. Greco/Roman
Female to Female to Male to Female Twice

An actress born in Baltimore, Maryland, 07/05/1877, who
had been a female writer in the Egyptian Ra-Ta period and
interpreter of poetry, law and songs for King Solomon,
entered as a male in Greece during the Greco/Roman
period when Grecians brought knowledge of interpretations
through drama, voice, and physical activities to Romans.

Romanos (Parceleus: Gk) [Male] - Grecian, beautiful in
body and abilities of interpreting drama through voice and
physical activities. 2598-2 F 64 - 3

►Bible Playbook◄

Study John 14-13, Deuteronomy 30
Study first, then, God's message to thee, as may be
interpreted in thy life from those records as have been made
and given for thy study [John 14-17]. Then manifest them

in thy experience. 2598-2

Study thoroughly Moses' last admonition, in the latter chapters, or thirtieth of Deuteronomy. Know that this means thee. 2598-2

Learn the 14th, 15th, 16th and 17th of John. Make those promises thine own. 2598-2

The Way, the Truth, the Light
DO write. DO talk. DO so live as to never condemn thyself, and to the glory of Him who is the way, the truth, the light [John 14:6]. 2598-2

Following that life, he was a noted female Barbara Frietchie [Fritchie?] during the early part of the American Revolution followed by the other female incarnation in 1877.

Thus the closeness the entity has felt and has held to the spiritual angles, and in the attempts to comprehend the messages many have attempted to unite with the entity's activity. 2598-2

Ye Shall Know the Truth...
Know that in Him may ye know the truth, the truth indeed that may set thee free [John 8:32] from thy wanderments, from thy activities that have at times brought disappointments. 2598-2

2. Greco-Roman
Female to Female to Male to Female Twice

An actress born in Montreal, Quebec, Canada, 10/25/1912, who had entered from an Atlantean urge and was a female in the Egyptian Ra-Ta period who assisted putting individuals "through paces" to determine latent and manifested factors for activities, especially the "fair sex"

Thus the entity is a fair judge of human nature, especially of others of its own ilk or sex. This is often resented by others. For, when those are met who were a part of the experience then, they clash again - as has been experienced by the entity time and again. Yet the abilities to control self, control self's emotions, control self's wants and desires, arise from that experience of the entity in the Egyptian period. 2950-1

She was next an artiste, actress and model in the Persian Uhjltd period followed by that in a changed sex in Greece the Greco/Roman period:

Echoras [Male] Brought Grecian stage influence to Romans. - 2950-1 F 30 – 3

Influences/Urges
We find the entity an Atlantean and a Uranian. And these indicate that the entity will in this experience either become one well known, and excel in many ways, or it may become the complete failure. 2950-1

►Bible Playbook◄

Walk In The Light of Him Who Is the Way
But never lose the confidence in self or self's abilities. For it appears that those extremes will be in the experience of the entity. But hold fast to thy faith in the DIVINE, and know that as ye walk in the light of Him who is the way, the truth and the light, [John 14:6] ye will find peace and that peace which comes from being as a channel of help for others. 2950-1

Following that experience he incarnated as females in

America when there was early consciousness of activity that later led to freedom of speech and activity among the "fair sex" before the one in Canada where she became an actress.

Answer to her query if she was wrong in hoping to combine material desire for fame, wealth and power, with her strong wish to serve others in the way she felt she could best do it best was:

Your Body Is the Temple of the Living God
Not thy will but His. Know indeed that thy body is the temple of the living God [1Cor. 6:19]. Give the credit to Him. Use thy abilities to the glory and honor of Him, and that will be to the honor of self. 2950-1

But know what ye believe. Analyze thyself, first, and thy hopes, desires, purposes. Know as to whether these are in keeping with the ideals thou hast chosen, with which or by which to conduct both thy spiritual and mental life. And keep that faith. 2950-1

Keep in those directions which will lead to a closer walk with Him.

Thy hopes may be attained to in material things, if ye learn to work with others. 2950-1

3. Greco-Roman
Female to Male to Female Twice

A female artist born in Chicago, Illinois, USA, 05/28/1923, who had been a female Emissary in Ancient Egypt during the Ra-Ta period, was a male in Greece during the Greco-Roman period when they were coordinating political and social activities with Rome:

Mazesra [Male] (Known as Rolo in Rome) Singer/actor - 5105-1 F 20 - 2

In the subsequent lives in England, Early America and in 1923, he incarnated as female.

►Bible Playbook◄

Study to Show Thyself Approved
Keep Self Unspotted From the World

Take warning from those things indicated as would not apply in the practical sense. Do apply self first in analyzing self. Know the relationships between physical, mental and spiritual attributes of body. Do know the ideals of the body and that to which it would attempt to attain. Then study to show thyself approved, a workman not ashamed, rightly dividing the words of truth [2Tim.2:15] and keeping self unspotted from the world and from condemnation [Jas. 1:27]. 5105-1

4 - Greco-Roman
Female to Female to Male to Female Three Times

A female composer born in Wapun, Wisconsin, 08/26/1872, who had been a female Atlantean leader of that group in sex and revelry in Egypt during the Ra-Ta Period and a female Bedouin, who composed music that aroused the spiritual-mental self to rehabilitate cellular forces within the system and the inner self in Persia during the Uhjltd period, entered as a Grecian in a changed sex in Rome during the classical period:

Quilla [Male] Grecian, active with Romans furthering experience of arts when those gifted translated story and song "to arouse within the lives and experiences of others an appreciation of the harmonious effect not only of verse or rhythm, but of activities of the body in association with same." 2131-1 F 67 - 3

Following that experience, he was again a female in England engaged in activities that presently bring the latent urge to write, and the one in 1872.

►Bible Playbook◄

With What Measure You Mete...
Thus it behooves the entity, in the present, not only to study to show self aware but capable of giving proper evaluations as to needs in the mental, the spiritual and the material experience of dealing with the fellow man. For with what measure you mete, it is measured to thee again [Mat. 7:2, Mk. 4:24, Luke 6:38]. Thus in whatever an entity may profess, the manners of activity bring about that, according to the consistency and persistency in same. 2131-1

Study to Show Thyself Approved Unto God
Then, as indicated, study to show self approved unto God, a workman not ashamed, and correctly dividing the words of truth [2Tim.2:15]. 2131-1

Many Have Entertained Angels Unaware
Then, in same, heed that injunction which may be a part of self: Be not unmindful to entertain those even who may appear not physically, mentally or materially necessary in thy experience. For many have entertained angels unaware [Heb. 13:2]. Also, be not unmindful that the manner in which ye meet the issues in thy relationships to thy fellow man is the manner of relationship that ye INWARDLY bear, as an entity, and manifest towards, thy Maker [Mat. 25:40, 45]. 2131-1

Day Unto Day Uttereth Speech…

The application of self in these directions brings the need of remembering: "Day unto day uttereth speech, night unto night sheweth knowledge" [Psa. 19:2]. 2131-1

Show Self Approved Unto God

As to the abilities of the entity in the present, and that to which the entity may attain, there come those ideas, those influences and forces as we have indicated. Hold fast [1Thes.5:21] to that which has been indicated should be, as it were, the chorus of the purposes and ideals, to show self approved unto God, a workman not ashamed [2Tim.2:15]. 2131-1

5. Greco-Roman
Female to Female to Male to Female Twice

An actress born in McAllen, Texas, 10/05/1912, who had been an Atlantean princess in Egypt during the Ra-Ta period, and an Indian female leader in the dance in Persia during the Uhjltd period, was next a male in Rome when attempts were made to embrace activities of Grecians in drama, games and oration:

Guilfuld [Male] Speaker, writer, beautiful in body, attraction for opposite sex brought turmoil- 2655-1F 29 -3

Advice/Abilities

And these may be met in the present experience by the inactivity that attracts when not meant to be." 2655-1

The abilities as the speaker, writer, also arise from that activity, as Guilfuld. In that experience the entity gained, the entity lost. 2655-1

And in the meeting of same in the present, keep thy judgments. 2655-1

Following the male incarnation in Rome he was a female Barnstormer in the US following reconstruction in 1812 and the one in 1912.

▶ Bible Playbook ◀

With The Measure You Mete...

These may be virtues or they may be faults. The sincerity, to be sure, is a virtue; but minimize the faults, magnify the virtues, as ye speak of others. For, with the measure ye mete it will be measured to thee again [Mat. 7:2, Mk. 4:24, Luke 6:38]. 2655-1

Let that mind be the builder that is the intuitive force for the Christlike hope of man [Phil. 2:5]. 2655-1

6. Greco-Roman
Female to Male to Female

A female born in Chicago, Illinois, 10/01/1920 that had been female in Egypt during the Ra-Ta period was next Grecian male in Rome when they were bringing Grecian philosophical teachings to Rome

Orian [Male] Representative of the court of Greece in preparing manner of greater continuity of body, how understanding of life might be obtained through study and application of tenets that told of man's relationship to Creative Forces, learned "the necessity of the requirements for cooperation among groups." 2872-3 F 23-2

Following that experience he changed sex and was female in early America during formation of groups whose tenets held to special dispensation of interpreting man's relationship to self and God.

▶Bible Playbook◀

The Lord thy God is one Lord
Thus the entity may act in the capacity of instructing others in the secret understanding of: The Lord thy God is one! [Deut. 6:4, Mk. 12:29] 2872-3

The abilities of the entity lie in choosing those ideals, not merely as something for others but as the attempt to apply in its own experience, its own active life, philosophy of the Orient. 2872-3

These are the more appealing to the entity and may be applied in the life, but know it is all inclusive in "Know ye, O Israel, the Lord thy God is one Lord" [Deut. 6:4, Mk. 12:29]. 2872-3

Answer to the question if her previous lives were the reason for her physical condition was:

Resentments in regard to those not thinking as self. In applying this then, it isn't indicated that the entity is to become so broadminded as not to be principled by ideals, but the ideal not ideas. The ideal must be one, even as He is one.
He Is Not a Respecter of Persons…
For He is not a respecter of persons [Acts 10:34, 2 Pet. 3:9], but did not will that any soul perish, but keepeth those who trusteth in Him. 2872-3

Answer to the questions of the purpose of her present incarnation and how she should go about getting work were biblical:

As Ye Do to Others, Ye Do To Thy Maker
Study the philosophical or theosophical data. Lecture. Most of all, study self. For if ye would know others, know self.

For as ye do to others, ye do to thy Maker [Mat. 25:40, Mat. 25:45]. 2872-3

The Still Small Voice Within

Apply self, rather, though, in these. Not being unto self, sufficient, but know that in self is the way to truth and light and understanding, and not that someone brings thee a message from heaven or from over the sea [Deut. 30:11-14] but as it answers to the still small voice within [1 Ki.19:12]. 2872-3

▶18◀
Roman Empire

1. Expansion
Female to Male to Female Twice

A female Quaker born in Wilmington, Ohio, 09/22/1893, who had been a female in Egypt during the Ra-Ta Period and in the Holy Land during the return from captivity under King Xerxes, was a male in Rome during the early periods of expansion:

Puella [Male] Among those sent to foreign lands to create constructiveness in environs "Hence the life during that experience was one of hardships physically, yet mentally and spiritually it was a growth throughout." 1620-2 F 44 -3

Following that life he incarnated as females in Early America and the one in 1893.

▶Bible Playbook◀

With What Measure Ye Mete...
It is well, then, that the entity take all of those inclinations as may be presented and analyze them within the

experience of self; and know that what is everyone's business is nobody's business. While, to be sure, it is well to analyze and to have advice or counsel from this or that student of this or that thought or activity, the real analysis must come from within. For it is with what measure ye mete that it is measured to thee again [Mat. 7:2, Mk. 4:24, Luke 6:38]. 1620-2

Study to Show Thyself Approved
Then, study to show thyself approved, a workman not ashamed; calling always upon that which is THY promise to Him that has promised thee! [2Tim.2:15]

Answer to whether she should sell the Scientific Treatise, "The Ultimate Particle," and what procedure to follow was:

As You Would That Men Should Do To You…
Find that within self, rather than through here. Apply that as has been indicated. Would you like for others to present it to thee? What is it to fill in the lives and the hearts of others? What has it filled in thee? Then the answer, "As ye would that men should do to you, do ye even so to them" [Mat. 7:12]. 1620-2

2. Expansion
Female to Male

A female newspaper reporter born in Peekskill, New York, USA 06/27/1898, who had the opportunity to run for Congress, but instead used her talents serving college girls, had been one of the wives chosen to care for the young in Egypt during the Ra-Ta period and one chosen as a female judge of the people from the tribe of Asher during the Exodus and wilderness period, was next a male when the Roman Empire was expanding:

Alamack [Male] Representative of Rome in Libya, served people well, had sense of justice, gained in favor in own land and with people he labored with 3486-1 F 45-3

Advice

As to the application of self through the sojourns in the earth, these necessarily may be brief, but the entity should apply self according to the application made in the Roman experience, as well as in the periods when the entity acted in the capacity, as one of the judges in the journey from Egypt to the Holy Land. 3486-1

▶Bible Playbook◀

Read Exodus19:5

Study those activities well, and remember to read and apply the 19th chapter of Exodus and the 5th verse [Exo. 19:5]. Know indeed, that shall be the basis of all thy undertaking. For as the promise is there, to each and every soul, do His biddings and ye will be a peculiar people to those that seek their material ways. 3486-1

Answer to her query of how to obtain the gift of inspirational writing in order to earn money to spend in educating a worthy boy or girl, or a tired mother with small babies was:

Read that indicated in the 5th verse of the 19th chapter of Exodus. ["Now therefore, if ye will obey my voice indeed, and keep my covenant, then ye shall be a peculiar treasure unto me above all people: for all the earth *is* mine: "] For all power comes from and through that source. 3486-1

As You Do Unto the Least of Your Brethren...

And these will be a part of the entity's activities in its choice as representative of the people, institutions, schools and the like, as the care for same. These stress in thy experience, not only as a reporter but as a representative of the people. For as ye do it unto the least of thy brethren, ye do it to thy Maker [Mat. 25:40, 45]. 3486-1

Who Is Your Brother?

In thy activity stress the care and attention to those in penal institutions, in the weak-minded, in the schools of correction, in the higher education if ye would contribute at this time to the welfare of thy state, thy nation, thy brothers. For who is thy brother? He that doeth the will of the Father [Mat. 12:50, Mk. 3:35]. 3486-1

Let Your Yeas, Be Yea ...

Let thy yeas, be yea and thy nays be nay [Mat. 5:37, Jas. 5:12] in the Lord, and let everything be done in decency and in order [1 Cor. 14:40]. 3486-1

Answer to her question: "What has been the reason for the experiences I have had for the past 25 years?" had universal application:

As Ye Meted It To Someone Else...

You are just meeting yourself. As ye meted it to someone else, it is being meted to you [Mat. 7:2, Mk. 4:24, Luke 6:38]. 3486-1

Answer to whether she has measured up to the test put to her and what she was meant to do in the future was also applicable to most:

Neither Do I Condemn Thee...

Judgments can only be in self. What is set as thy ideal? For nothing passes judgment. "Neither do I condemn thee" [John 8:11] has ever been the word of the Master before whom we must be judged as individuals. For the way ye treat others is the way ye will be treated. Be patient, and in patience ye will find your soul [Luke 21:19]. 3486-1

The familiar Biblical quote on personal retribution given in response to her question on staying healthy applied to her trinity:

As Ye Sow, So Shall Ye Reap

As ye sow, so shall ye reap [Gal. 6:7] - in body, in mind, in spirit. 3486-1

1. Roman Empire - Augustus Caesar
Female to Female to Male to Female Twice

A female editor born in New York, New York, 01/19/1891, who had been a female datastician in Ancient Egypt during the Ra-Ta period and in Persia during the Uhjltd period changed sex and was a male in Rome when Augustus Caesar made changes in relationships of various groups under the empire:

Millincus **[Male]** Historian, gave people new interpretation of activities, needs, abilities of groups, provinces, and people of different religions on how to live together as contribution to welfare of earth - 2830-2 F 52

Following that incarnation, he was a female in early America during reconstruction after the revolution that ministered to needs of the young, and again in 1891.

►Bible Playbook◄

A Little Leaven…
…the entity is as the leaven that may leaven the whole lump [1 Cor. 5:6, Gal. 5:9]. Here a little, there a little [Isa.

28:10, Isa. 28:13], does the entity influence those with whom it comes in contact day by day. 2830-2

The Way, the Truth, the Light
… the Creative Force made or brought into being SOULS to be equal with, and one with, Him; even as is manifested in the Way, the Truth, [John 14:6] the Light. 2830-2

To Whom Much Has Been Given…
Remember, as first indicated, thy abilities are many. Of him to whom much has been given is much required [Luke 12:48]. 2830

Study to Show Thyself Approved
Know in what ye believe, but know also the author of thy faith [Heb. 12:2], the author of thy confidences; and study to show thyself approved [2Tim.2:15] unto thy ideal. 2830-2

Bless Those Who Despitefully Use You
Condemn not, and bless those even who would despitefully use thee [Mat. 5:44, Luke 6:28]. 2830-2

As You Do Unto The Least Of Them…
For, inasmuch as ye do it unto the least of thy brethren, ye do it to thy Maker [Mat. 25 40, 45]. 2830-2

You Body Is the Temple of the Living God
Thy body is indeed the temple of the living God [1 Cor. 6:19]. There He has promised to meet thee. Meditate oft in same. 2830-2

Be not afraid
Be not afraid of His directing care, His directing voice [Mat. 14:27, Mk. 6:50, John 6:20]. 2830-2

Answer to the query if she could be of the most service by remaining in her present position, also included symbolic Biblical imagery:

As we find, in the present and for the next few years, yes. Keep the interests, of course, in nature, and in nature's storehouse. Keep close to the earth oft; with the feet well on the ground, but look to the mountain. For the mount is the hill of God. 2830-2

He Is Able To Keep That Committed Unto Him
Know thy purposes, and know thy authority for thy purposes. And know, be persuaded, [2Tim.1:12] in the spiritual, He is able to keep that committed unto Him against any experience that may arise in thy relationships with others. 2830-2

Light of the World
Let that light guide thee which has been the light of men since He gave, "God said, Let there be light, and there was light" [Gen. 1:3]. That light ye may know, for it is the light of the world, even in Jesus the Christ [John 8:12, John 14:6]. 2830-2

▶19◀
New Testament

1. Early Christian Era
Female to Female to Male to Female Twice

A female born in New York, New York, 02/11/1877 that had been a Princess in Atlantis just prior to second division and a female in the household of Pharaoh in Egypt during the raising up of Joseph, was male in Rome during the Early Christian era:

Pharlos [Male] Roman judge in Holy Land, later became associated with Cornelius [1848], advanced, returned to Rome when emperors changed, became active in home office when greater activities of new sect began. 2612-1 F 64 - 3

Following that incarnation, he was female in returns in Early New York before the revolution and the one in 1877.

Influences/Urges
As to urges arising from sojourns in the earth, and the indwelling through the periods of activity in other dimensions, we find latent and manifested forces according to that the entity cultivates within itself. 2612-1

▶Bible Playbook◀

Circumstances alter conditions in a material plane, but the spiritual and mental growth may not be altered. For, only self may keep the entity from fulfilling those purposes for which it entered the material experience in the present. [See Rom. 8:38-39] 2612-1

The Spirit Is Willing, But the Flesh Is Weak
And the purpose of each soul's entrance is to magnify the creative forces in the associations with its fellow men....The heart of most individuals is to do good; the spirit is willing, but the flesh is weak [Mat. 26:41, Mk. 14:38]. 2612-1

As to the abilities of the entity in the present, that to which it may attain, and how:

Study to Show Thyself Approved Unto God
Analyze first self, and self's desires. Then study to show thyself approved unto God, a workman not ashamed, but rightly dividing the words of truth [2Tim.2:15]; putting

stress upon essentials, leaving off those that would make afraid. 2612-1

▶20◀

Pre-Columbian

1. Norse Voyages
Female to Female to Male to Female

A female secretary born in Chicago, Illinois on 04/12/1908, who had been a female Libyan during the Ra-Ta period in Egypt and an Indian princess in Persia during the Uhjltd period, changed sex and was male when Norse were overrunning the Huns [German land]:

Heldaoslem [Male] One to be feared, led own group - 2995-1 F 35- 3

Influences/Urges
The entity materially gained, and yet is still fighting self in the lack of patience. It has the persistence, but learn indeed what is the difference between patience and persistence. There's almost as much as there is between personality and individuality. 2995-1

▶Bible Playbook◀

In Patience You Become Aware of Your Soul
Know that in patience ye become aware of thy soul [Luke 21:19]. And thy body and thy mind, and thy soul, are one. They live together. 2995-1

Your personality, then, is the material expression; and your individuality is the personality of the soul. 2995-1

Following that experience he was next females in Early Dearborn, Ohio and the one in 1908.

Only Self Can Separate You from the Love of God

For, nothing in heaven or hell may separate thee from the love of God, [Rom. 8:38-39] as is manifested in thy being, save thyself. 2995-1

With What Measure You Mete...

In judgment, as in mental self, it must be exacting, but no more exacting of others than of self, and no more exacting of self than of others. For, know, with what measure ye mete to others ye are measuring to thy Maker, God [Mat. 7:2, Mk. 4:24, Luke 6:38]. 2995-1

Your Body Is the Temple of the Living God

Know that all the creative force ye may become aware of is within thine own self. For, as thy body is indeed the temple of the living God, [1 Cor. 6:19] there He has promised to meet thee. 2995-1

The Word Is Already In Your Own Heart

And, as has been given by the law-giver of old, think not who will descend from heaven to bring you a message; for, Lo, it is already in thine own heart. It is thyself, thy inner self, thy soul self. Think not who will come from over the waters, nor over the seas to bring a message, for it is with thee already [Deut. 30:11-14]. 2995-1

If God Be With You, Who Can Be Against You

Do not think in self as to how ye may take advantage of someone else, or how ye may attain fame or glory. For these are thine own already. For if God be with thee, who can be against thee? [Mat. 12:30, Rom. 8:31] 2995-1

Art thou with Him? This ye ask and may ask and find within self. For, as He has given, "If ye call I will hear."

And He has promised to meet thee within thine inner self. 2995-1

Then in prayer, in meditation, in longing, in hoping, but in doing the things and being the things in thine inner self ye hope for and long for, these are the manners and the ways of approach, and of overcoming those tendencies which arise in the emotions. 2995-1

The Earth Is the Lord's And The Fullness Thereof
Not as one to be long-faced. For, the earth is the Lord's and the fullness thereof [Psa. 24:1, 1 Cor. 10:26, 28] - in JOY! 2995-1

Rejoice With Them That Rejoice...
Do not see the dark side too oft. Turn it over there's another side to every question. Cultivate in self humor, wit. Ye enjoy it in others, others enjoy it in thee. But too oft it becomes to thee foolishness. KNOW that thy Lord, thy God, LAUGHED even at the Cross. For He wept with those who wept, and rejoiced with those who rejoiced [Rom. 12:15]. 2995-1

2. Norse Voyages
Female to Male to Female Twice

A female born in Detroit, Michigan, 10/27/1887, who had been a female vocational counselor in Egypt during the Ra-Ta period, was next male in Norway during the early expeditions to other lands from which she gained a love of travel, adventure, and things having to do with interesting facts about individuals , peoples, organizations or activities:

Saeahdevien [Male] Seaman, acted with various groups meeting problems when changes were made to sea-faring activities, contributed to own land - 3000-2 F 55 – 2

Analysis/Bible Playbook

Do not feel that because some of those things, some of those activities have to do with animate and almost inanimate influences that these haven't the sanction of the Creative forces, or God. For, every thought must be accounted for [See Mat. 5:26] in man, or children of men. And every activity of a thing or a condition is an expression of someone propagating same, or from influences within or without that would glorify that experience of that force or entity. 3000-2

Following that male incarnation, he was females in early America when there were changes in the area between Toledo and Detroit and in the one in 1887.

Choose Thou

As to the abilities of the entity in the present, that to which it may attain, and how:

First, know thyself. Know thy activities, as to whether these are contributing to the ideal thou hast set for thyself or not. Choose thou [Jos. 24 15] as the power and the might of the individual is such, from the gift of the Creator, that it may make itself of itself amenable to suggestive forces from without as well as within. 3000-2

Your Body Is the Temple of the Living God

But know that thine own body is the temple of the living God [1 Cor. 6:19], not that as may manifest through the entity. 3000-2

Hence choose rather those tenets that are set forth so thoroughly in the 30th of Deuteronomy, and as verified by the teachings of the Master in the sermon on the mount as well as those especially in the 14th, 15th, 16th, and 17th of John where promises are given individuals. 3000-2

But do write at times of thy own experiences, rather than of those that would enslave thee in their own weaknesses. For, He has promised to be with those that seek His biddings. Know He is not far from thee, daily. 3000-2

Let Your Light So Shine Before Men
Let thy light so shine that others, seeing, may take hope, and may walk the closer with the Creative Force, God." 3000-2 [Mat. 5:16]

Answer to her question about what mistakes she is making in living was:

Who is to judge? Know thine own ideal, spiritually, mentally, materially, and then let thy life be an example of that ideal; keeping the faith with thyself, with thy fellow man. 3000-2

As You Do Unto The Least Of Your Brethren...
Know, as ye do it unto the least of thy brethren, ye do to thy maker [Mat. 25:40, 45]. 3000-2

Answer to her query about identity of entity putting her into hypnotic sleep at night was:

In My Father's House Are Many Mansions
Beware of *those* influences that would prevent thee from being thine own self. Walk closer with those forces as promised in, "In my Father's house are many mansions..." [John 14:2]. 3000-2

3. Norse Voyages
Female to Male to Female Twice

A female teacher born in Pittsburgh, Pennsylvania, 12/20/1902, who had been a female cousin of Ra-Ta in the

Egyptian period and a female among sages in Carmel during the expectancy of the coming of the Prince of Peace, was next an Earl in England during the period of turmoil from the Norse and Spanish:

Crumpet [Male] Earl, leader given grants in area of Northumberland "gained abilities as well as tendencies to be curbed within self" 2520-1 F 38-4

Advice
Keep that which is good, magnify that which is helpful in the experience of self as well as in others. 2520-1

Following that incarnation he changed sex and entered as a female in America during Early Settlings, establishing refugee camps along the Monongahela after the destruction of Ft. Dearborn, and the one in 1902.

▶21◀
The Crusades

1. Crusades
Female to Female to Male to Female

A female writer, born in Villa Rica, Georgia, 06/23/1896, who had been females in Egypt during the Ra-Ta period and in Greece during the time of Xenophon, was a male during the Crusades to the Holy Land with Bruce and failure of conquest:

Cordelli [Male] Crusader, learned lessons under Moslems who nursed him - 0696-1 F 38-3

Abilities/Influences/Urges
For the succor, the aid given by those people in that particular experience has brought to the entity in the

present sojourn the abilities to listen to many and to give, as it were, the place of others as to THEIR thought, as to their intent and their purpose. Hence again from these influences do we find the entity thrown upon the influences within the self inspirationally or intuitively for its abilities to allow others to give their own expression, their own beliefs. Hence FREEDOM for all, in thought, in activity, whether it be in the mental, the spiritual, the social or the moral life, in the activities of whatever sphere that may be the promptings provided the promptings are from within, and the entity or group find same constructive in the experience. 0696-1

Following that experience, he incarnated as females in Early America and the later one in Georgia in 1896

2. Crusades - England
Female to Female to Male to Female Twice

A female born in Barre, Vermont, 04/02/1890 that appeared as females in Egypt during the Ra-Ta period and in Palestine during the expectancy of the birth of the Messiah, was a male in England during the period of the first Crusade to the Holy Land:

Cushings [Male] (because of desire to manifest that activity). Became aware of brotherly love manifested by one considered religious enemy - 2173-1 F 50-3

Ability
In the present, from the lesson gained in that sojourn, we find the ability to apply not by might or power, but by "my word" gentleness, kindness, longsuffering, patience, those things called the fruit of the spirit, or having within them the spirit of the Creative Forces or Energies we call God, in such a manner as to bring into the hearts and

experiences of others the knowledge of the ONENESS of souls' relationships to the Godhead. 2173-1

Following the experience as a Crusader, he returned as females in early Virginia and the one in 1890.

► Bible Playbook ◄

He That Is Greatest...
We find that the experience through the earth's sojourn has never been one that might be termed as a bed of roses, or of splendor; yet rarely (save mentally) one of great want as to physical things or conditions; yet the entity in some experiences has made of itself a servant.

And, He gave that the one who would be the greatest among his fellows would be the servant of all [Mat. 20:27, Mat. 23:11, Mk. 10:44]. 2173-1

Few realize as this entity that no one individual may have too many friends; that neither is there any individual who has so many friends that it can afford to lose one! 2173-1

The Still Small Voice
Too much stress could not be placed on this, for in same may the entity indeed find that harmony which comes from such experience and application, in that it is not those who seek to do some great deed, or to arouse some throng to such an activity as to revolutionize, but Lo as has been ever given it is not in the tempest nor in the storm, but rather in the still small voice [I Ki. 19:12]. 2173-1

In Patience Possess Ye Your Souls
And this may be aroused by a kindly deed, a gentle word spoken when there is turmoil or strife, a brotherly hand held out, patience which the entity must learn; with that

appreciation of the beauty in its life, in its experience, and in patience ye will glimpse indeed thine own soul [Luke 21:19] and its growth in the presence of thy Maker. 2173-1

Thy Body Is the Temple of the Living God
Let NO thought ever divert thee from that as ye manifested there. Let not intellectual reasoning, as is sometimes called, dissuade thee from the trust in that birthright which is promised and given to each soul; that indeed thy body is the temple of the living God [1 Cor. 6:19], and that there, in thy holy of holies, He will meet thee and His promises do not fail. 2173-1

Let Your Yeas Be Yeas and Your Nays Be Nay
Then clutter not thy temple with strange fires, nor with undue vows, nor with strange offerings; but let thy yeas be yea and thy nays be nay [Mat. 5:37, Jas. 5:12], IN the Lord! 2173-1

Behold I Stand at the Door and Knock
Hold fast to that thou hast purposed in thy heart. Look ever, and oft, within for thy direction. Be satisfied with nothing less than knowing, as has been indicated, that He is mindful of thee. Then, speak as face to face. For the promise has been, and is, "I stand at the door and knock. If ye will open, I will enter, and I and the Father will abide with thee" [Rev. 3:20]. 2173-1

He Is With You Always
This applies to thee, not as a laudation over others, but humbleness of heart, humbleness in thy speech and thy conversation. And lo, He is with thee always, even unto the end of the earth! [Mat. 28:20]. 2173-1

3. Crusades - England
Female to Female to Male to Female Twice

A female born in Newport, Virginia, 04/20/1916, who had been females in Egypt during the Ra-Ta period and in Palestine when the Master walked in the earth, was a male in the English land during the Crusades, which was brought about by desires from the Palestine period:

> **Jorgas Bruce [Male]** Led young and old in cause he thought right, had unusual awakening in meeting that for which he stood - 2448-2 F 25- 3

►Bible Playbook◄

Not By Might nor By Power, but By Spirit
In the experience the entity suffered physically, yet in its inner self there were the desires for might and power and physical ability to meet emergencies. There was that determination (though delicate in body as in the present) which brought the experience of the stalwart Bruce; who found that "it is not by might nor by power, but by my spirit, saith the Lord of hosts" [Zech. 4:6]. 2448-2

What Ye Sow Ye Also Reap
For, know that what is TRULY thine CANNOT be taken away from thee; nor is any real character ever lost.

Remember these, not merely as axioms, but in analyzing the happenings through the sojourns in the earth:

Be mindful of the manner of seed ye sow.   For, what ye sow ye also reap [Gal. 6:7]. 2448-2

With What Measure You Mete...
With what measure ye mete, it is measured to thee again [Mat. 7:2, Mk. 4:24, Luke 6:38].

If ye would have love, be lovely to all. For, in the manner ye meet and ye act toward others, ye are measuring and meting to thy Maker. 2448-2

Your Body Is the Temple of the Holy Ghost

Know that there is only one Spirit, and that thou possessest thy measure of same. Thy WILL is given thee to use or abuse that Spirit. For, the Spirit is of the Creator, and thy body is the temple of that Spirit [1 Cor. 6:19] manifested in the earth to defend or to use in thine own ego, or thine own self-indulgence, or to thine own glory, OR unto the glory of Him who gave thee life and immortality if ye preserve that life, that spirit in Him. 2448-2

Whatsoever a Man Sows...

Oft has the entity found that so many disappointments appear in others. Know that first rule, a LAW that is eternal: The seed sown must one day be reaped [Gal. 6:7]. Ye disappointed others. Today from thine own disappointments ye may learn patience, the most beautiful of all virtues and the least understood! 2448-2

He Came Unto His Own...

Remember, it is one of the phases or dimensions through which thy soul may catch the greatest and the more beautiful glimpse of the Creator. For, as He came unto His own and His own received Him not [John 1:11], in patience He brought that awareness of what they had lost in their lack of appreciation of the opportunities given. 2448-2

Let Not Thy Heart Be Troubled

Let not thy heart be troubled [John 14:1]; ye believe in God, believe also in Him who is able to quicken the life as it flows through thy body, thy mind, thy soul, to a full regeneration in the material world, then hope in the mental, then truth in the spiritual. For, He IS truth, and the light, the way [John 14:6]; that each soul may find the way from the darkness back to God even as He. 2448-2

There Is A Way Which Seems Right Unto A Man...

With its abilities and its analytical mind, the entity innately sees those records upon that scroll. Yet there is the sense of a judgment, as indicated in that seal; that there is a way which seemeth right unto a man, yet the end thereof is first disappointment, then fear and doubt, and then separation, withering away [Prov. 14:12, 16:25]. 2448-2

Overcome Evil with Good

Be not overcome of evil, but overcome evil with good [Rom. 12:21]. Know that a smile will rally many to thy cause, while a frown would drive all away. 2448-2

Following that male experience, he incarnated as females in Colonial Williamsburg, Virginia as companion of Governor Dunmore and the one in Newport, Virginia in 1916.

4. Crusades - France
Female Who Had Been Male During Crusades

A female born in Hertford Co., North Carolina, 04/16/1911, who had been females in Atlantis, in Egypt during the Ra-Ta period and in Persia during the Uhjltd period, was a male in France during the Second Crusade to the Holy Land before returning as females during the American Civil War and the one in 1911:

Richelleneaux [Male] Leader of Spanish and part of German and French forces, rose to power and might - 0263-4 (15) F 42 - 4

►Bible Playbook◄

He is the Way, the Vine
First find self and know what and who and in whom thou wouldst believe, to whom thou would serve, and why and whether these be for the spirit of the Law of One or for the aggrandizement of self's own individual self. For as ye chose in that experience in Atlantis BOTH WAYS, these will be thy experience in the present. Meet them ONLY, and they may only be met in Him who is the author, the maker of light, life and immortality in that He came that man in the flesh might know the way.

For He IS the way [John 14:6], the water of life, the vine, and men and women are the branches [John 15:1-8] if they are grounded in Him. If they take root in the earth for their OWN dependence, it must become as tares that must be rooted out. 263-4

Study to Show Yourself Approved
Then, study to show self approved unto Him [2Tim. 2:15], WITH Him. 263-4

If Ye Love Me Keep My Commandments
For as thou hast had power, might, in the earth; so in Him in the earth may ye again make for that of an awakening in self, in others, as to those truths that, "If ye love me and keep my commandments, I will come and abide with thee [John 14:21], that thou mightest have that power in the earth as was GIVEN thee in the beginning." 263-4

Answer to the query if she was psychic and, if so, how to develop it for greater use, applied to everyone:

He Will Bring All Things to Your Remembrance
Every soul is psychic, and the entity is above the ordinary from the experience. The abilities have been used erringly. Turn them to the light. Let the light of the truth guide thee, as in His promises that "I will abide with thee and bring to

thy remembrance ALL THINGS from the beginning" [John 14:26]. 263-4

Then meditate upon that the Lord thy God, thy Christ, would have thee do. Let thy prayer day by day be:

Prayer
Here am I, Lord! Purge thou me from all unrighteousness. Make me a greater channel of blessings to everyone day by day; not my will but thine. O Lord, be done in and through me. 263-4

5. Crusades - France/Germany
Female to Male to Female Twice

A female born in Lexington, Missouri, 05/04/1901, who had been a female during the Ra-Ta period in Egypt, was a male during the French/German Crusades before returning as females with first settlers in Missouri and again in 1901:

Simeon Ardienned [Male] - Leader in Crusade. placed little value on life, which became too often the impelling force in the present. 1336-1 F 35 - 2

►Bible Playbook◄

As Ye Sow, So Must Ye Reap
Hence the spiritual import for those things is, "As ye sow, so must ye reap" [Gal. 6:7]. 1336-1

In Him You Live and Move...
As to the gain or the loss, it depends in the present upon whether or not the spiritual force or God is taken into account with same. If not, ye cannot walk the way alone; for it is in Him that ye live and move and have thy being! [Acts 17:28] 1336-1

6. Crusades - France
Female to Female to Male to Female Twice

A female born in New York City, 03/17/1883, who had been females in Atlantis and in Persia during the Uhjltd period, was a male in France during the Crusades to the Holy Land for an idea before returning to New York as a female during the first settlings and in 1883:

Jaun Bettelli [Male] - Crusader, not so much out of sincerity for cause as for expediency and exploitation, reached Turkey, was captured and injured, changed when ministered to by those he avowed to destroy, returned to Cannes applying great commandment and golden rule - 1599-1 F 54-3

Innate Forces
And from that experience there arises within the INNATE forces of the entity in the present the ability in a psychic nature; the ability to be AROUSED! Yet how have ye used that? or how MAY ye use that? 1599-1

For remember, as given, ye are constantly meeting thyself! 1599-1

From the activities in that experience, if ye will meditate the more upon how that as He gave, love and forgiveness, faith and hope may overcome spites, fears, distrust, ye may open thy heart, ye may open thyself to the opportunities that CONSTANTLY lie before thee in thy activities in the present. 1599-1

►Bible Playbook◄

Depart From Me, I Never Knew You
If these are to be used for self-aggrandizement, self-indulgences, do they not become rather as He gave of old?

"Ye shall come and say, Did we not in thy name heal the sick? did we not in thy name cast out demons?" and He will say, "Depart from me, I never knew you!" [Mat. 7:22-23] Why? WHY? 1599-1

He That Would Be the Greatest…

Because the desire, the purpose is that self may be exalted, rather than the humbleness of the heart before Him. For he that would be the greatest must be the servant of all [Mat. 20:27; 23:11, Mk. 10:44]. 1599-1

Choose Thou

THESE be those things that ye must choose within thine own experience. 1599-1

For there is ever, as given of old, set before thee each day good and evil, life and death choose thou! [Deut. 30:15, Jos. 24:15] 1599-1

These are not, then, other than that thy prayer should ever be: 1599-1

Prayer - Use Me As Thou Sees Fit

Lord, here am I Use me in the way THOU seest that I may be the greater channel of blessings to those I meet day by day. 1599-1

For until ye are willing to LOSE thyself in service, ye may not indeed know that peace which He has promised to give to all. 1599-1

My Peace I Leave With You

For as he gave, "My peace I leave with you my peace I GIVE unto you." Not as the world giveth peace [John 14:27], but that which is able to keep thee ever as in the shadow of His wing. 1599-1

In Patience You Possess Your Soul
As to the appearances in the earth, then, we find these quite varying in the environs as well as the inclinations that have been brought into the emotions of the ENTITY in the present. 1599-1

And those influences in the emotions, unless they be governed by an ideal, often may become as a stumbling-stone. 1599-1

But use rather thy choices, thy endeavors, thy experiences, in a way and manner that they may become stepping-stones for a greater comprehension, a greater awakening of that consciousness of the Creative Forces of good, of hope, of faith, of brotherly love, of kindness, of gentleness; yea, of patience. 1599-1

For too oft have ye lost thy concept of what patience means! And as He gave, "In PATIENCE become ye AWARE of your souls!" [Luke 21:19] 1599-1

The Great Commandment
For as He has given, the whole law is to love the Father in mind, in body, in soul and thy neighbor as thyself [Mat. 22:37-39; Mk. 12:30-31, Luke 10:27]. 1599-1

These are ONE. There are no preferences before Him, save they that love His ways for they are a part of HIM, that do such. 1599-1

Love Thy Neighbor as Thyself
There, on the return, the entity made the greater practical applications of those tenets with which it had started forth, or for which it had started forth: Love thy neighbor as thyself, and as ye would that men should do to you, do ye even so to them [Mat. 7:12]. 1599-1

With What Measure You Mete...

We find that in the present the entity may apply the tenets of that experience, if it will turn to those influences that come to the entity from the application of self in meting to others that "ye would have measured to thee" [Mat. 25:40, 45, Mk. 4:24, Luke 6:38].

For as ye have done and as ye do it unto the least, ye do it unto thy god-self as well as thy Maker. 1599-1

For those laws are as immutable as Life itself, that as ye measure to others so is it meted to thee. For as ye have done and as ye do it unto the least, ye do it unto thy god-self as well as thy Maker. And ye become in same that as hinders or that as a growth. 1599-1

Lord thy God is ONE

...there ARE abilities as in each soul - to become indeed the true child of the living God; in that thine own self is a manifestation of His love. 1599-1

Why WHY not express same in thy dealings with thy fellow man?

First there must be the finding of self, then; realizing there cannot be one relation with thy fellow man and another with thy Maker, not one expressed in words and another lived in the inner life. 1599-1

But know "Know O Israel the Lord thy God is ONE!" [Deut. 6:4; Mk. 12:29] 1599-1

These sounded, these kept within, ye may rise to those abilities to give, to measure out, to become a channel through which many may call thee blessed! 1599-1

Study then to know thy relationship to thy Maker. But
KNOW WHO is thy Lord, thy God! 1599-1

Answer to her query about what would be the best
metaphysical studies applied to all was:

Study John 14-17
Fourteenth, fifteenth, sixteenth, seventeenth of John! [John
14-17] and put thyself in same! Know that He is speaking
to THEE! 1599-1

7. Crusades - France
Female Four times to Male to Female Twice

A female born in Norfolk, Virginia, 07/19/1919 who had
been a daughter of Ra-Ta in ancient Egypt, a daughter of
Ishmael in the Holy land, a princess in the Gobi Land
during the time of Zend, and a niece of Joseph in Palestine
following activities of the Prince of Peace, was a male in
France during the Crusades:

Renee Charleveauxr [Male] - Leader in Crusades
(Overshadowed in present by misdirected intents and
purposes in the Holy Land.) 1709-3 F 20 – 5

▶ Bible Playbook◀

He Hath Not Willed That Any Soul Should Perish
For He hath not willed that any soul should perish, but has
with every temptation prepared a way, a manner of escape
[1 Cor. 10:13, 2 Pet. 3:9]. And the more oft it comes
through thy friends, thy associates. And as these have been
and are oft representative of a savior, a means, a manner, a
way, so must ye in thy association and thy activity make of
thyself as one that would be a help, a savior, an aid, a
HOPE for many. 1709-3

For As Ye Sow, So Must Ye Reap
For as ye sow, so must ye reap [Gal. 6:7]. 1709-3

Following the incarnation as a male, he experienced conflict as a female in Virginia during the Civil war before the one in Norfolk.

The Lord thy God is One
There we find that the entity was disturbed through the activities or conditions, and the hopes that were shattered during those influences. These brought materially the disappointing influences in the experience, yet INNATELY brought a depth of desire, or an innate desire for knowledge, for understanding, for a broader concept of the whole, - and the realization of that greater law which, if there is the full expression or experience of same, may arouse each soul to its greater expression or manifestation, - "The Lord thy God is One!" [Deut. 6:4, Mk. 12:29] All force, all power emanates from that which is allowed or directed by or through Him, - according to thy purpose. 1709-3

He That Would Be the Greatest Of All
Measure in this experience that as ye would have measured to thee. Learn the lesson that ye failed to learn in that experience, that ye or she that would be the greatest among thy fellows, thy associates, will serve them all [Mat. 20:27, Mat. 23:11, Mk. 10:44]. 1709-3

8. Crusades - France
Female to Female to Male to Female Twice

A female born in Buenos Aires, Argentina, 05/08/1908 who had been females in the Ra-Ta period in ancient Egypt and in Argentina when the Incas journeyed to the land, was a male in France during the Crusades to the Holy Land

Crusader [Male] Choice to make sure of relationships with companion in her activity and experience [chastity belt?] brought hardship upon her and material separations (Created karmic condition to be met in next appearance.) 2281-1 F 32 – 3

►Bible Playbook◄

There Is A Way That Seems Right unto Man
Thus in the present the entity is meeting itself, in that it chose rather to make such a hardship upon its companion that it brought material separations in the experience; and in that activity the entity learned much that will be met in the present. There is a way that seemeth right unto a man, but the end thereof is death [Prov.14:12, 16:25], disillusionment, separation. That ye have learned, that ye must apply in thy present experience. 2281-1

Following that incarnation, he was female during the period of reconstruction from the American Revolution before the one in 1908.

The advice and biblical playbook given for this soul has a general application:

For, each soul comes into experience not merely by chance but that it, the soul, may have the opportunity to be an expression, a manifestation of that force called God, in materiality. 2281-1

He Hath Not Willed That Any Soul Should Perish
For He hath not willed that any soul should perish, but hath given with every temptation [1 Cor. 10:13, 2 Pet. 3:9], with every trial, that strength, that peace, that harmony which if grasped hold of makes all trials and temptations to be stepping-stones to a greater awakening, a greater awareness

to the beauties and joys that await those who love the Lord and His coming. 2281-1

Judge Not That Ye Be Not Judged
So, with this entity, though the burdens and the trials have at times become heavy, and though they may become heavy at the suddenness, the unusualness of the character or kind of trial, let there be no temptation for blame. Judge not that ye be not judged; for with what judgment ye mete to thy fellow men it shall be meted to thee again [Mat. 7:1-2, Mk. 4:24, Luke 6:37-38]. 2281-1

Let Your Yeas Be Yea and Your Nays Be Nays
Let thy yeas be yea and thy nays be nay, in the Lord [Mat. 5:37, Jas. 5:12].

In Him We Live and Move and Have Our Being
For in Him alone ye live and move and have thy being [Acts 17:28].

The Lord Is In His Holy Temple
While for the time there may be shadows that cause doubt and fear, know that the Lord is in His holy temple; [Hab. 2:20] and keep ye quiet, calm within, if ye would hear and know His voice as He speaks with thee. 2281-1

In My Father's House Are Many Mansions
In the astrological aspects we find Venus as both the benevolent and the tragic influence in thy experience. For, in love, in the joy of loving, in the passion both innate and manifested, there have been and are the emotions of the body, as well as in the sorrows, the dreads that have arisen and do arise from same. Yet know, even as He has given, in thy Father's house are many promises of the mansions [John 14:2] that ye shall know and shall enjoy in welldoing. For, if there is not good in thy activities, in thy living and in thy experiences, know that sin comes before thee; but thou

shalt choose as to which way ye shall take. 2281-1

Your Body Is the Temple of the Living God
For, thy body is indeed the temple of the living God [1 Cor. 6:19], and there He has promised to meet thee.

Ask and You Shall Receive
And as ye meditate, as ye pray within thy inner self, ask and ye shall receive [John 16:24]; knock and ye shall not be empty but supplied with that love, that harmony which is the promise of Him who has given, "If ye love me, keep my commandments, and I will come and abide with thee" [John 14:21].

If The Lord Is With You...
And if ye find the Lord is with thee, who can be against thee? [Mat. 12:30, Rom. 8:31] 2281-1

...that which appeareth not is more sure, to those who love the Lord and His ways and His coming, than those things which partake of the earth as earthly things. 2281-1

Know In Whom You Believed
Hence these are not to be condemned, but rather cherished, in that they take hold upon self in such a way that ye KNOW in Whom ye have believed, and that He is able to keep that which has been and is promised unto thee day by day [2Tim.1:12]. 2281-1

Rejoice With Them That Rejoice...
Thus, be ever as a messenger, as an entity or individual that makes known the ways of the LORD! not as one that would be long-faced, or that would separate self from others so much. For, be even as He, who was known among those of every estate, dining with those who dined, weeping with those who wept [Rom. 12:15]; among the poor to cherish them, among the rich to give that as needed for their

activities among their fellow men. 2281-1

As to the abilities of the entity in the present, these may be limited only by the ideal or the purpose the entity sets for self. 2281-1

Wait On the Lord
Love ye the Lord and wait ye on him continuously [Psa. 27:14, Psa. 37:34, Prov. 20:22]. 2281-1

Response to her query if she would be well-off or continue as she was presently was that she would be: Well off financially; for the laborer is worthy of his hire.

The Earth Is the Lord's...
The earth is the Lord's and the fullness thereof [Psa. 24:1, 1 Cor. 10:26, 28].

The Silver and Gold... are His
The silver and the gold and the cattle on a thousand hills are His [Hag. 2:8, Psa. 50:10]. If ye would serve Him, these may be thine even as they were when ye served thine own peoples so well in thine own land; as ye did even when thy life was prolonged by the cutting short of certain influences in thy experience in France. 2281-1

9. Crusades - France
Female Four Times to Male to Female Twice

A female born in Bennington, Vermont, 07/30/1921 that had been a Priestess in Atlantis just before the first destruction, a granddaughter of Ra-Ta in Ancient Egypt, a female musician in Persia during the Uhjltd period, and a female drama/dance assistant in Greece was next a male in France during the Crusades:

Crusader [Male] Made overtures as leader of a group - 2700-1 F 20 - 5

Advice
Here indeed may it be said, know first thy ideal, physical, mental and spiritual. Each phase of thy experience bears one upon the other, yet these are influenced definitely in the experience. 2700-1

Following this incarnation, he entered again as females in Colonial New York, Mohawk Valley and the one in 1921.

►Bible Playbook◄

It Is More Blessed To Give Than To Receive
Hence there would be needs of the systematic reactions, for little of system though routine oft becomes a part of the entity's experience, but little of systematic routine is deeply motivating the influences to that of bringing security at periods. However, it is true that those who open not to give to others neither open to receive the greater blessings [Acts 20:35]. 2700-1

The Spirit Is Willing, But the Flesh Is Weak
There are the needs of a protecting force. Yet know that there is the power latent within self that may ever be the guiding light. For, spirit is willing, flesh is weak [Mat. 26:41, Mk. 14:38]. Motivated by the influences of the spirit there may be brought the promptings of the heart and the mind not only material but mental and material satisfaction, and spiritual strength, in this material plane. 2700-1

Study to Show Yourself Approved
But study to show thyself approved [2Tim.2:15] unto the ideal chosen. Keep self in body, in mind, TRUE to that

ideal; keeping self away from harsh judgments of others. 2700-1

With What Judgment You Judge...
For, with what judgment ye judge, ye shall be judged thyself. [Mat. 7:1-2, Luke 6:37] 2700-1

10. Crusades - France
Female to Male to Female Twice

A female born near Mt. Pleasant, Pennsylvania, 08/08/1888, who had been a female in Spain when Atlanteans were taking refuge, was a male in France during the Crusades.

Schmellenzar [Male] Crusader, discovered his fault only when kindness was shown by those considered heathens, breakers of the law, eventually embraced different principles in relationships to worship - 3574-2 F 55 – 2

►Bible Playbook◄

He Is the Same Yesterday, Today and Forever
Thus the entity finds itself unstable as to what is to the entity truth indeed. Truth is the unalterable, unchangeable law, ever. What is truth? Law! What is Law? Love. What is love? God. What is God? Law and love. These are as the cycle of truth itself. And wherever ye are, in whatever clime, it's ever the same. For, as it is said of him, He is the same yesterday, today and forever unalterable! [Heb. 13:8] 3574-2

I AM THAT I AM!
Not as the Medes and Persians that were built upon fallible conditions, but as: I AM THAT I AM! [Exo. 3:14] That is true. Search it in thy inner self. Cultivate it in thy mind and

it will alter the results in thy physical being. Yes, ye will have much to live for. For everyone will be your friend, as ye have something to give to everyone. Not as that which brings fault or brings want, and indeed makes an individual poor, but that which is a blessing to the mind and to the soul, by giving grains of truth that take from no one, but add something to everyone. 3574-2

Following that incarnation, he was female in early America among the Quakers in the one in 1888.

The Peace That Passes Understanding

The entity was among those who helped to apply the tenets and truths, but when there was unfaithfulness in the relationships because of neglect, it brought doubts and fears and eventually the condemning of self. Hence in the present ye find unfaithfulness, as ye proclaim, in others near to thee. These are the reflections of thine own doings. Love them! Not in the manner that ye embrace them, but know that which is endeared to thee, by the very activities, may bring a peace that passeth understanding [Phil. 4:7]. These are lessons to learn. 3574-2

Study: Deuteronomy 30, Romans 3 and John 14

Right about face in thine own concept or application of the concept of things of the spirit. Read very carefully the 30th of Deuteronomy. Compare it with the things Paul indicated in the 3rd of the Romans. Then turn to John 14, and there find thy self, and the relationship to the Maker. Thus ye will find greater joy in living, greater harmony in the experience may be thine. 3574-2

Let the law of the Lord direct thee. 3574-2

11. Crusades - Germany
Female to Female to Male to Female Twice

A female born in Solingen, Rhineland, Germany, 01/12/189, who had been a female artist/teacher during the Ra-Ta period in Egypt and a female weaver/baker in Persia during the overrunning by the Greeks, was a male in Germany during early period of Crusades to Holy Land, Turkey, Macedonia:

Wilbenstrauss [Male] Crusader, among few who returned, associate of current son, came in contact with those of a different faith, of tenets that had not been understood - 0718-2 F 42 -3

Determining Forces
And with the changes wrought, it brought the determining forces that later brought about a great many changes in the activities of the entity in its influence upon those things in its native land, as it returned. 718-2

In the latter part the entity gained; for its activities in making for the united efforts on the part of groups brought about the greater material, mental and spiritual development. Yet it altered the entity's stress upon spiritual things, as ordinarily termed. But spirituality and spiritual things may be entirely different, if the stresses will be put in their proper place. 718-2

►Bible Playbook◄

Study To Show Thyself Approved Unto God
Study then, first, to show thyself approved unto God; then a workman not ashamed [2Tim.2:15]. 718-2

►22-◄
Journeys to New World

1. Journeys
Female Three Times to Male to Female

A female born in Wurttemberg, Schwabesch Gmud, Germany, 10/30/1884, who had first been a female in the Ra-Ta period in Egypt, where she studied to show herself approved [2Tim.2:15 Jas. 1:27] in the Holy Land during the return from captivity, and in Germany during period of expansions in the land, was next a male in England when Cabots were settling, before returning as a female in Germany:

> **Henrico Deuen [Male]** In crew of the Cabots, remained, became active force, went through hardships, but gained because of trueness to self and sincerity of purpose that others may know the true and living God - 4055-2 F 59-4

Urges
These as we find as urges latent and manifested. These, then, we would give that the entity analyze and study within self: 4055-2

▶ Bible Playbook ◀
Thinking Highly of Self
There is little the entity may not accomplish if it sets its own mind and head and heart to do so. These are the inclinations for the entity to think more highly of its judgments than sometimes others think of same [Rom. 12:3]. This is not a reprimand, rather as the warning. For without an exalted thought of self, but in accord with God's purposes, who will think better of thee? 4055-2

2. Journeys
Female to Female to Male to Female Twice

A female born in Marquez, Texas, 09/11/1900 that had also been female in Egypt during the Exodus was next a male in England when there were journeys to the New World, before entering as a female in 1900:

Henry Narravarre [Male] Kept log of journeys of a crew, laborer in various soils, was overbearing - 5258-1 F 43- 2

▶ Bible Playbook ◀

Study to Show Thyself Approved Unto God - Keep Self Unspotted From the World

As to the abilities of the entity and that to which it may attain; study first thyself and thy relationships to the Creative Forces, and then keep self unspotted from the world or of condemnation of others [2Tim.2:15, Jas. 1:27]. 5258-1

▶ 23 ◀
English Restoration
1. Charles II, Oliver Cromwell
Female to Female to Male to Female Twice

A female born in Portsmouth, Ohio, 01/02/1910 that had been an Atlantean during the Ra-Ta period in Egypt and a relay runner/model for Mercury in the Greco/Roman period of the games was next a male in France when Charles II was in exile and Cromwell was in England:

Dubuquer [Male] Associated with king's household, involved in breaking down religious fervor that brought Cromwell to activities and reestablishing of Charles II to English throne, became soldier of fortune after Charles rose to power and lost interest in him - 0934-1 F 24 - 3

This incarnation was followed by two female appearances: one in Ft. Dearborn and the one in 1910.

▶ Bible Playbook ◀

Answer to her query "Which previous incarnations are to influence me the most during the next few years?" included a biblical quote:

In Him We Live

As indicated, it may be all or none, dependent upon the choice of those urges that come from WITHIN; for many have been the planetary or sojourning urges that make for many of the experiences that arise within the present experience or sojourn. And what they cause depends upon that which becomes or is INNATELY and APPLICABLY the urge that PROMPTS same. If it is for self-indulgence, for self-exaltation, then it becomes as that which will eventually bring ITS reward. If it is for the glorification of the Spirit of Truth, those influences that make for Life itself as creative energies that are of the constructive forces, then these within the next two and a half to three and a half years will make for that which will with the using of its knowledges, and knowledge from the Atlantean experience and those experiences in the various activities as indicated bring the greater mental development, and the greater satisfaction. For know, ye live and move and have thy being in Him [Acts 17:28]. If thou dost exalt self, thou dost crucify thy Lord. If thou dost exalt thy Lord, thou dost bring peace and joy and happiness into thine life. 0934-1

▶ 24 ◀
Early America

1. Settlings
Female Three Times to Male to Female

A female chiropractor, naturopath, born in Warrington, England, 05/20/1897 that had been a female in Gobi Land during the Ra-Ta period in Egypt, a female Samaritan in

Palestine during the Return from Captivity with Nehemiah, and a female in England during the First Crusade, was a male who came to Early America with Hardcastle, who followed Smith:

James Buhanan [Male] - Freebooter, freethinker, came with Hardcastle, traveled colonies obtaining sustenance from indigenous people and others, associate of Emily Carllton [1402As] in English-ruled New York, gained through a life spent in mental application -1397-1 F 58 - 4

Innate Influences
In those activities especially where there was the obtaining from the natives, as well as others, that which made for bringing bodily strength, the influences to keep that balance between the mental activity, did the entity make for those experiences in that sojourn. 1397-1
From the experience, we find these as innate, these as emotions for the entity: To try those things new, yet holding to those things proven; yet trying those things that may be in combination of the two as related to activity in individual lives. 1397-1

Healing is a portion of, a part of the entity's experience through the sojourns in the earth. While the application of self in these directions has at times brought those influences and forces that have caused questionings on the part of some as to the manner in which such applications were influencing, and do influence, the lives of others. 1397-1

►Bible Playbook◄
Hence there still remains not merely what may be termed karmic influences, if one were - or the entity were - to define such in its own experience. For under material law one meets that it has constantly sown, but if constructive

influences or forces of Creative Energies are applied, these become rather as null in the experience. 1397-1

Woe to the Man by Whom Offences Come
For it indeed becomes as has been given by Him of old, it must needs be that offences come, but woe to him by whom they come! [Mat. 18:7, Luke 17:1] 1397-1

An Eye for an Eye, a Tooth for a Tooth
Hence because an offence may have been committed against thee, only in attempting to demand an eye for an eye, a tooth for a tooth [Mat. 5:38], or blood for blood, does one become only under the law. 1397-1

But doing good for evil, being gentle when harshness is manifested, makes for that attunement to the influences within the soul as well as in the experience of an entity in material activity, of harmony and peace and quiet. 1397-1

Whatsoever a Man Sows...
One may not sow riots and reap harmony. One may not sow [Gal. 6:7] indiscretions of any nature and expect the mental, the physical or the spiritual to respond as an instrument attuned to only good. 1397-1

Study to Show Self Approved
Hence first study to show self approved [2Tim.2:15] unto that the self has set and does set as an ideal. 1397-1

That Ye Sow, That Ye Reap
In the present that as indicated: That ye sow, that ye reap [Gal. 6:7]; that ye MUST learn! 1397-1

Mercy, And Not Sacrifice
For evil may not be done that good may come; whether it is in what may be termed a karmic force or not. For these continue to make for barriers that must be brought to not

sacrifice but mercy [Hos. 6:6, Mat. 12:7, Mat. 9:13], not justice as upon the law but grace that ye may have and ye may make in the experience of all those influences that may bring the better forces for constructive increase in the experiences of others. 1397-1

Study to Show Thyself Approved
Answer to her question regarding past associations with her partner, who has apparently become unfriendly, and how to handle the situation to their mutual advantage was:

Then, studying to show thyself approved [2Tim.2:15] unto same, never making for that questioning in self or of others as to their purposes - so long as they are constructive. 1397-1

Do Unto Other...
...Do unto the other person as ye would have him do to you [Mat. 7:12]. Study his relationships. 1397-1

These relations or associations arise from the period when destructive forces came into thine experience, or during the Crusades; yet these are to be worked out. How? 1397-1

2. Settlings
Female to Female Twice to Male to Female

A female Protestant Office Clerk, born in Buffalo, New York, 07/04/1898, who had been a female in Egypt during the Ra-Ta period, in Persia during the Uhjltd Period and in Rome during the early Christian era, was male in Early America when settlers were pushing inland from Eastern Shore before returning as a female:

Jean Nathanson [Male] - Teacher/minister, born in land, gained by giving aid and help to others, lost in the material experiences for self-aggrandizement - 2144-1 F 41 - 4

►Bible Playbook◄

Study to Show Thyself Approved
Yet study to show thyself in thy activities, in thy thoughts approved [2Tim.2:15] unto that thou hast chosen, or may choose, as thy ideal. And in the ideal, know that it is not as to what one may attain only, but as to what may be spiritual, mental and material ideals. 2144-1

In Your Patience Possess Ye Your Souls
Faint not at waiting, for in patience ye become aware of thy soul. [Luke 21:19]

3. Settlings
Female to Female Twice to Male to Female

A female Protestant Secretary born in 1899?, who had been a female in Egypt during the Ra-Ta period, a female in the house of Zerubbabel in the Holy Land during the return from captivity and in France among the wives left behind during the Crusades, was a male in Early America when there was the first establishing of a great deal of shipping, importing and exporting before returning as a female:

Amos Dowell [Male] In shipping import/export business, encountered controversial conditions concerning regarding "who was to supply the channels for activity, as well as to who was to be paid for gathering the materials that were shipped." - 2116-2 F 41- 4

►Bible Playbook◄

As You Sow, So shall You Reap
Then, detail at times becomes drudgery, yet the entity requires a great deal of same within its own experience. But, learn the law as to that ye sow being also that ye must

reap [Gal. 6:7]. Ye cannot build upon those influences in the experience to the detriment of another. For the law of the Lord is perfect, and it adjusts, it brings the cooperative forces in the activity in EVERY phase of the life. Just as it is necessary for the better influences of the body for each organ to coordinate with another, so must the purposes and the relationships with individuals; and NOT as were some portions of the entity's activities in those periods, as Amos Dowell. 2116-2

Know In What You Have Believed
In that experience the entity lost, the entity gained, the entity lost. Thus we find fears, doubts oft arise, even to that point to which the entity may distrust itself. But know rather in what ye have believed, and who is the author of same [2Tim.1:12], and that he is able to keep thee through any experience. Such ye will find in the study, yea, the application, of those tenets presented by Him in HIS relationships to man and to the world! 2116-2

Grow In Grace, In Knowledge
For, each soul manifests that it may become a channel through which there may be expressed the ideal which is set in creative energies and forces as manifested in the man Jesus. So may each soul grow in grace, in knowledge [2 Pet. 3:18], in understanding. For, His promises are sure; to those who walk in that way in which the life, the manifestations in relationships to others, bring hope and creative forces of a spiritual import in the experience of self and others. 2116-2

4. Settlings
Female to Female Twice to Male to Female

A female Christian born on Tutuila Island, Samoa, 11/23/1905, who had been females in Egypt during the Ra-Ta Period, in the Holy Land during the first return from captivity and in Rome during the reign of Claudius Caesar, was male in America when the navy was being established before the one in Samoa:

John Vel Heilder [Male] Naval officer, commanded "aided in bringing about the first of those activities that brought to the peoples of this land an ideal as to activities of officers as well as men in service in the U.S. Navy." 1201-2 F 31- 4

Influence
In the experience from the mental the entity gained; from the material and spiritual, so much of that as has to be overcome in the present is from those very inmost experiences of the entity. 1201-2

►Advice-Bible Playbook◄

For each soul is constantly meeting itself, and only self may separate the understanding from the Creative Forces [Rom. 8:38-39] that bring harmony, joy, peace, yea happiness into the experience of each soul if it will but accord itself to being good for something, rather than just being good or just going along gaining or taking or with the "gimme's" from all the associations and activities. 1201-2

In Patience Do You Possess Your Souls
LEARN YE PATIENCE, if ye would have an understanding, if ye would gain harmony and grace in this experience! "For in patience do ye possess your souls" [Luke 21:19]. It's when individuals have become impatient, and desire their own will or desire their expression or desire that they as individuals be heard, that they become less and less in that close association with the Divine and more of that as is human and of the animal becomes manifest. This is a power, to be sure, but fraught with egotism becomes a destructive power. 1201-2

And bad is only good gone wrong, or going away from God. 1201-2

Study First To Show Yourself Approved
As to the abilities then in the present, and that to which it may attain, and how:

Study first to show thyself approved [2Tim.2:15] unto an ideal that is not of the earth but spiritual. And ye may read same in the psalms that thou hast sang so well. Ye may know them in the music and the art of nature itself, as it brings harmony in the experiences of individuals and groups and nations. And see the good; not the coarse, nor that which breaks up harmony. 1201-2

Your Body Is the Temple of the Holy Ghost
For the Lord is in His holy temple, His holy tabernacle; and thy body is that temple [1 Cor. 6:19], that tabernacle. Make thy body, thy mind, harmonious with the songs of nature, the songs of the artists that would depict the love of God or of the Creator for His creature; and ye will find peace and harmony becoming so much a portion of self that thy expression of life itself will become glorious in its experience. 1201-2

1. Salem Witch Hunts
Female to Female to Male to Female

A Catholic female Telegrapher born in Boston, Massachusetts, 02/10/1893 that had been a female Indian sent to Egypt for study during the Ra-Ta period and a female Grecian in Persia during the Uhjltd period, was a male in Salem, Massachusetts during the periods of the witch hunt persecutions before returning as a female in 1893:

Boodie [Male] In ecclesiastical court, controlled minister in church, gained through the assistance and aid given to many that were persecuted for the convictions in their own conscience, yet lost by holding grudges at times when those persecuted became violent 0338-2 (4) F 40-3

►Bible Playbook◄

Study to Show Self Approved
Hence, study first to show self approved [2Tim.2:15] unto Him from whence all power emanates, realizing that each activity that becomes manifest in the earth is a reflection (and not the thing itself) OF that One Power. For, man's MENTAL being may only take hold upon that power which emanates from Creative Forces themselves. Hence it is ever high, yet becomes manifest in that individuals do and create IN the lives of their associates through the mental and material contact. 338-2

Keep true, then, to self; setting the ideal in Him that is the pattern, AFTER the pattern SHOWN thee in the mount! 338-2

His Ways Are Not Past Finding Out
Be NOT overcome by censure, nor too easily guided by public opinion. Harken more to those periods when, in vision, in dream, there is presented to self that which opens more and more the mental associations of self with the Creative influences in the world. For, God IS! Ye that seek Him may find Him, for His ways are not past finding out to those who put their trust in Him!" [Rom. 11:33] 338-2

►25◄
Revolutionary

1. American Revolution
Female to Female to Male to Female

A female born in Virginia in 1886, who had been a female in Egypt during the Ra-Ta Period whose name meant, "the dual life as One," and was the woman who touched the hem of Jesus' garment and was healed [Mat. 9:20-22], was male in early Williamsburg, Washington, Richmond, and Fredericksburg during the American Revolutionary War period:

Clarence Fairchild - Leader, physically incapacitated, but prompted others to activity 1353-1 F 50 -3

► Bible Playbook ◄

He That Would Be the Greatest...
Hence these shall be ever as the promptings - the freedom of the soul, of the mind. IN Christ! These are not as gloryings, not as those forces that make for indulgences, nor of laudation; but rather as He - in humbleness of heart. For he that would be the greatest among you is the servant of all [Mat. 20:27, Mat. 23:11, Mk. 10:44]. 1353-1

Know In What You Have Believed
First, know in what ye have believed [2Tim.1:12], knowing He is able to keep that committed unto thee against any experience that may arise in the material world. For if ye are His, then let Him guide, let Him direct. 1353-1

Answer to her query of any spiritual advice was:

Study to Show Thyself Approved...
Study to show thyself approved [2Tim.2:15] unto Him who is the Light [John 1:4-9, 1Jn. 1:7], and the Way {John

14:6]; who stands at thine OWN door, as to all, and knocks [Rev. 3:20].

Keep Self Unspotted From the World When You Call...

Then as ye study, divide the words of truth in their PROPER relationships, keeping self unspotted from the world [Jas. 1:27]. 1353-1

For He having blessed thee, ye cannot wander far afield - if ye will open thy consciousness to His abiding presence.

For as He hath given, "When ye call, I will hear."

2. The French Revolution
Female to Female Twice to Male to Female

A female born in St. Albans, Vermont, 05/15/1878, who had been females in the Ra-Ta period in Egypt, in Persia during the Uhjltd period, and in Indo-China during the period of descendants of Mu and Saneid was a male in France when there was the formation of influences that impelled activities of groups and masses [Revolution?]

Charlean Heltzlett [Male] Lecturer, advocate of nationalist movement 1847-1 F 60 - 4

Innate Influence
Hence all things pertaining to that land are INNATELY a part of the entity 1847-1

And the arousing of the emotions comes through the very influences and forces as experienced and manifested during that particular experience. 1847-1

►Bible Playbook◄

As one thinks in the Heart, So is He

As we find, as indicated by those of the period, while astrological aspects are not as ordinarily indicated by the manner the entity has applied self in the present experience to the mental and material environs, these show indications, as from the sojourn of the entity in those environs which are accredited with such influences. For as one thinketh in the heart, so do such influences become active in the entity's experience [Prov. 23:7]. 1847-1

Study First To Show Thyself Approved

As to the experience in the present and the application of self, as to the abilities and the meeting of self in the influences as may be wrought: 1847-1

Study first to show thyself approved [2Tim.2:15] unto that thou hast set as thine ideal. Know these are found in man's attempt to seek the closer relationship with the Creative Forces or the sources of his material sojourn; and that only in the applying of same in the MATERIAL things, as in relation one to another, may these become a part of the experience of all. 1847-1

www.ingramcontent.com/pod-product-compliance
Lightning Source LLC
LaVergne TN
LVHW051840080426
835512LV00018B/2979